"*The fecundity of an author can be gauged by the ferti*
and the richness of the solutions their thinking makes a
this prism that one should approach this masterful new
tour of some of his core preoccupations, from the peculia
phenomenon of evacuative manifestations. The unifyi
voice and style of thinking, suffused in equal parts with his Bionian background and his own
liveliness, clarity and creativity."

–**Elias da Rocha Barros**, Training Analyst, Sao Paulo Psychoanalytic
Society, Brazil; Fellow, British Psychoanalytic Society

"*Nino Ferro's talent is inimitable. This new book is full of subtle clinical examples demonstrates
his imaginative skill and deep playfulness, squiggling with serious intent and an unparalleled
sensitivity to the complex field of human interaction in the clinical setting.*"

–**David Tuckett**, Training and Supervising Psychoanalyst, British
Psychoanalytical Society; Professor and Director of the Centre for the
Study of Decision-Making Uncertainty, Psychoanalysis Unit,
University College London, UK

"*Antonino Ferro invites to think differently by offering us a rich book, generous of examples of
his way of swimming in the field co-created by the analyst and the analysand. His perspective
moves away from content to address the process and the tools available for dreaming, thinking
and feeling. If he walks in the footsteps of the Baranger and Bion, he is distinctively himself
with his own style of walking and deepening the exploration. Dr. Ferro gives us a stimulating
example of how psychoanalysis remains in movement!*"

–**Martin Gauthier**, Training Analyst, Canadian Psychoanalytic Society;
Child Psychiatrist, McGill University, Canada

PSYCHOANALYSIS AND DREAMS

Psychoanalysis and Dreams explores some of the cornerstones of Antonino Ferro's theoretical model but also attempts to extend the dreamlike boundaries of the model. Based on Bion's theory of alpha function and the analytic field, Ferro has developed his own original theorization of transformations in dreams and of work in the analytic session as a waking dream.

Clearly highlighted in the book is Ferro's theory that transformation in dreams is the activity which is constantly carried out in the mind of the analyst, who nullifies the reality-status of the patient's communication and considers the patient's narrative as a dream which must be constructed in real time in the encounter between the two minds at work. At the centre of his theoretical proposal stands the transition from a psychoanalysis of contents to a psychoanalysis which develops the apparatus for thinking, based on the conception of an unconscious in a perennial state of construction and transformation, which must be dreamed, and which continuously expands as it is dreamed.

Psychoanalysis and Dreams is written for practicing and training psychoanalysts, psychotherapists and psychiatrists and will be helpful in everyday psychoanalytic and psychotherapeutic work.

Antonino Ferro is a training and supervising analyst in the Italian Psychoanalytical Society (SPI), of which he is the former president, the American Psychoanalytic Association, and the International Psychoanalytical Association (IPA). He has been a visiting professor of psychoanalysis in various institutions in Europe, North America, South America and Australia. He received the Sigourney Award in 2007.

BY THE SAME AUTHOR

The Bipersonal Field: Experiences in Child Analysis

In the Analyst's Consulting Room

Psychoanalysis as Therapy and Story Telling

Seeds of Illness, Seeds of Recovery

Mind works. Technique and Creativity in Psychoanalysis

Avoiding Emotions, Living Emotions

Torments of the Soul

PSYCHOANALYSIS AND DREAMS

Bion, the Field and the Viscera of the Mind

Antonino Ferro

Routledge
Taylor & Francis Group

LONDON AND NEW YORK

First published 2019
by Routledge
2 Park Square, Milton Park, Abingdon, Oxon OX14 4RN

and by Routledge
52 Vanderbilt Avenue, New York, NY 10017

Routledge is an imprint of the Taylor & Francis Group, an informa business

This book is a translation of a work previously published in Italian by Raffaello Cortina Editore Srl as Le Viscere della Mente: Sillabario emotive e narrazioni (2014).

Translated by Adam Elgar.

British Library Cataloguing in Publication Data
A catalogue record for this book is available from the British Library

Library of Congress Cataloging-in-Publication Data
A catalog record for this book has been requested

ISBN: 978-0-367-15019-8 (hbk)
ISBN: 978-0-367-15020-4 (pbk)
ISBN: 978-0-429-05451-8 (ebk)

Typeset in Bembo
by Taylor & Francis Books

MIX
Paper from
responsible sources
FSC   FSC® C013056
www.fsc.org

Printed and bound in Great Britain by
TJ International Ltd, Padstow, Cornwall

To Claudio, Eugenio, Glen, Jim, Tom.
To the members of the Pavia Psychoanalytic Centre.
To all those who do not think like me, with gratitude.

CONTENTS

1 Swimming to the fundamental rule   1

Introduction 1
Clinical reflections 5
The magic filter: contributions from Bion and from field theory 9
Conclusion 11

2 Denial, negative capabilities and creativity   13

Introduction 13
A look at the relational dimension 14
Play and negative capabilities as an antidote to denial 15
The interpretative line 16
Verbal squiggling 20
Transformations in play 21
Operations upstream of interpretation 22
Negative capabilities and creativity in the session 22

3 Making the best of a bad job: Research in the consulting room   28

Premise: what kinds of research exist today in psychoanalysis? 28
A little map for finding my way 29
What subjects for research have most intrigued me? 30
How do we position ourselves, so as not to be alone? 31
But this is not psychoanalysis 39

4 What's hard to talk about and often gets said in whispers   42

   And the poor wretch replied! 42
   What do trainee analysts say when they do feel able to speak? 45
   Get thee behind me, Satan! 46
   The vertex of dream-listening: film and session as dream 47
   Fear and psychoanalysis 51
   The white coat and neutrality 53

5 Evacuative and psychosomatic pathologies: In the light of a
   post-Bionian model of the mind   55

   Introduction 55
   Bion 56
   Analytic field 59
   Dyslexia, enuresis, elective mutism 62

6 Weaving thoughts and images in my own way   65

   Introduction 65
   Work in progress 69
   From O to K: the oneiric column of the lie 71
   Circular time and linear time 72
   In praise of lying 74

7 On the subject of supervisions   75

   Group supervision 75
   Individual supervision 78
   Opening blocked passages: aka, the WD40 function 80

8 Theorising through practice   86

   *Dreams and their capacity for poetic syncretisation: the "derelict" house
    and the eyesore 86*
   Evacuations 87
   Sexual disturbances 88
   Listening to the patient and the magic filter 89

9 Gradients of alphabetisation   96

   Introduction 96
   Potential criminality (delinquency) 102
   Disturbances in learning 103
   Casting the characters 104

Row C of the Grid 105
Depression 109
The dilapidated bell-tower 114

10   Random thoughts on technique and other matters   116

Contents and modalities: what film are we going to see? 116
The field 119
The psychoanalytic church: or fear 119
Traumas 122
Biological markers of time and connected defences 123
A digression about dreaming 124

References   *136*
Index   *140*

1

SWIMMING TO THE FUNDAMENTAL RULE

Introduction

In the history of psychoanalytic technique, the "fundamental rule" has had an immeasurable importance, because it establishes the mental setting in which patients have to find their way. "The analysand is asked to say what he thinks and feels, selecting nothing and omitting nothing from what comes into his mind, even where this seems to him unpleasant to have to communicate, ridiculous, devoid of interest or irrelevant" (Laplanche and Pontalis, 1967).

"Say whatever goes through your mind": this is followed in Freud's text by the metaphor of the traveller in a train telling whoever he is sharing the compartment with about the changing landscape outside. This in turn is followed by the request for sincerity and a number of other suggestions.

I think that when psychoanalysis was being born, and its method was very little known, there was a need for "regulation" and for simple, unambiguous rules of conduct, and so, as a result, such communications were totally necessary.

I remember that when I started working as an analyst I too gave these instructions to the patient, in an ever more simplified form as the years went by; whereas now – on the whole – I do not provide these rules, for several reasons.

Nowadays I find it, on the one hand, a highly prescriptive and superegoistical approach and, on the other, one very much based on the attention being addressed to the patient's mental functioning (or rather, the way in which the patient "should" communicate), whereas today I would tend to consider that the mental and communicative functioning is co-generated by the way the analyst presents himself, including mentally.

I think the method of functioning "by free association" is a point to aim for, and one not to be reached immediately, in the development of something to which the analyst also contributes: hence the title of this chapter, borrowed from a book on dyslexia that was famous in Italy during the nineteen-eighties (Bing, 1976).

Now, once we have come to the first session, if there is a very long silence or a difficulty on the part of the patient, only then do I intervene, often a highly unsaturated way, with "What then?" or alternatively, "Naturally you can tell me what's passing through your mind", and sometimes with an interpretation of the atmosphere that seems to be being created.

A while ago, a writer – I don't remember who – made a collection of all the ways in which the principal novels of world literature begin, and – again I don't remember whether it was the same writer or not – a collection of all the ways of ending a novel.

With the development of analysis – while always standing on Freud's shoulders and being grateful to him – I think we can give up the metaphor of the chess game in which the opening and closing moves are the only acceptable steps in a "systematic presentation": I would also give up the "certainty" of these moves, in the sense that I think every analysis can open and close in its own way (as can every session); over the years I have seen that there is an extreme variability of styles in this area too.

In narratology, the name "encyclopaedia" is given to the totality of knowledges that we have acquired about the functioning of a text. Hence, a highly saturated encyclopaedia stops us having the taste for the co-construction of the text, putting us into an anticipatory bottleneck (the paradoxical extreme case of which would be that it was always the butler who did it); whereas having an unsaturated reference to "encyclopaedias" and to "possible worlds" makes us open to unforeseen and unprecedented narratives.

I think I would interpret the patient's way of communicating/not communicating and these narrative modes insofar as they become a problem, having in mind a series of precise facts. In fact, a range of different lines of development will take shape in this context.

- The analyst's ability to be "without memory and desire" (Bion, 1970), in the sense of not having expectations or predictions about the stories that will come to life (Freud speaks indirectly about this when he tells us that there will be greater difficulties to address if the patient is the child of friends or acquaintances, or if there are some lines of development already determined by prior knowledge). This mental state is not easy because we feel a whole set of internal and external pressures strongly imposing themselves on us.
- The analyst's *negative capability* (Bion, 1963): that is, the ability described by Bion to tolerate being in a paranoid-schizoid (PS) position without persecution, until one can direct oneself towards a selected fact, as in cat's cradle game, in which a different figure is defined depending on which part of the string we unhook. Closely connected to this are the qualities of analytic listening, which would be open to all the possible variations I have described in the oscillations between "grasping" and "casting" (Ferro, 2008; 2009). But "What does the analyst listen to?": Grotstein's (2009) reply is blunt: the analyst must "listen to the unconscious".

- But how do we conceive of the unconscious? As described by Freud, by Klein, or by Lacan? Naturally, we could embark on a long digression about how Bion (1962; 1992) understood the unconscious, and many with him from Grotstein (2007; 2009) to Ogden (1994; 2009), and how this new conceptualisation may revolutionise the very way in which we conceive the field, as I shall say below.
- The analyst's *capacity for rêverie*, that is his capacity to transform into images the elements of sensoriality deriving from the situation and from the analytic atmosphere, a topic too well known to be dwelt on here.
- The different way in which, right from the start, we will consider the *characters* (Ferro, 2009) who come into the session: characters from history, characters from the internal world, hologram-characters reflecting the functioning of the analytic field (Ferro and Basile, 2009).
- The type of *interpretative "response"*, verbal, silent, acted or countertransferential, made by the analyst to the patient's first communication. Naturally, here we come across the enormous problem of how to validate the interpretation: two points I would like to emphasise are, first, Bion speaking of the "patient as our best colleague" and hence as the person who always knows what is in our mind (Bion, 1983; 2005), and that of the patient considered as a satellite navigation system, who unconsciously "dreams" his response to the interpretations, thereby constantly giving us the location of the analytic situation.

To sum up, I am not saying that the analytic rule must not be stated, but stressing that it is a multifaceted question, which has much more complex effects than we may have believed, and is much less neutral than we had thought; in some ways it is even a sort of self-disclosure of the analyst's desires and expectations. It is often a destination, otherwise the possibility of being accepted and respected would become a serious "crux" in relation to the criteria of analysability.

It is as if a canvas could give information about how it is to be painted: what would become of paintings by Fontana or others in which the canvas is torn all the way to the frame, or those paintings in which the frame itself "explodes"? And why must the analysis have the immediate flavour of a confession in which it is a "sin" to leave out things that one isn't ready to share? And why should we remain seated by the window commentating if, for example, there is a fire? And if the flames reached the train and the compartment? And if one of the passengers pulled out a pistol, or a knife? And what if a Rottweiler came in? And what if there was a robber, or one of the passengers died?

I shall stop here, but I could go on *ad infinitum*, without even mentioning child analysis or the analysis of patients with severe pathologies (borderline, psychotic, etc.). And what are we to do with a compliant or Zelig-like patient?

And what should we think of the "promise of absolute sincerity" which ends up shutting off an infinity of possible worlds and narratives?

We would end up laying down excessively strict rules which would put a straitjacket, or at least a corset, on the patient's freedom of expression, which remains free as long as it is not excessively codified. It will be different if, instead of being a sacred rule, it is passed through the analyst's mental functioning, or takes the form of metaphors such as "airport duty free", or of the analysis as a place where one pays no import duty and any *game* is permitted.

Naturally, there is then the problem of what model the analyst has of the analytic process. For example, if after the "fundamental rule" has been communicated, a patient were to say, "It reminds me of when I was at school and the priest told us how we should behave", would this be a memory that opens up a scenario of the analysis or would it describe the patient's emotional state, feeling himself to be in a religious school with rules for behaviour?

Or if another patient said, "I remember that when I was a child, I held back my faeces; I wanted to go, but I couldn't", would this be another possible opening deriving from infancy, or is the patient transmitting his present difficulty in communicating what he is holding back, *malgré soi*?

Or if, as soon as the rule has been communicated, a patient tells his dream of a terrifying wolf behind him, which he is afraid will sink its fangs into him – is this the opening scenario that would have unfolded in any case, starting off his analysis, or is it the description of how he has experienced that communication, as threatening, dangerous, lacerating?

But what do I mean by calling it a question of models?

In a model inspired by Freud, it will be a matter of working on resistances, repressions, memories, and traumatic events, and the characters will to a great extent refer to the patient's history. Attention to the historical reconstruction, to the collateral transferences, and to the analyst's free-floating attention will be some of the main tools which will permit access to the unconscious, above all by means of improvised ideas ("*Einfälle*"). A model inspired by Bion will see things differently: turbulences, storms of sensoriality will be transformed by the alpha function (which is always at work) into sequences of pictograms (alpha elements) which will constitute the "waking dream thought", and the aim of the analysis will, above all, be the development of this dream-thinking, and of yet more tools for generating it (alpha function and ♀♂); or else the *dreaming ensemble* (Grotstein, 2007) will be central, in the form of rêverie, of transformations in dream (Ferro, 2009), and of *talking as dreaming* (Ogden, 2007).

Viewed in this light, free associations will no longer be free, but will be obligatory associations (although with freedom in the choice of narrative genre) in terms of the formation of that particular waking dream sequence that is in itself unknowable, but whose derivatives, however distorted, are knowable (Ferro, 2002a; 2006a).

Another key point is to consider a unipersonal model or a relational model, or even a field in which every character, not necessarily anthropomorphic, describes the functioning in place between the minds of patient and analyst, or rather it is a fragment – it would be better to say, a derivative – of their dream-functioning.

In this sense, the session becomes a dream shared by the two minds, to which the analyst will contribute with rêverie and with negative rêverie (–R), broadening or restricting the field.

In conclusion, I believe that the "fundamental rule" of being in contact with one's own unconscious and communicating it, must be a co-constructed destination, experienced to an ever greater degree session by session.

Clinical reflections

Between Barbie and nun

After a brief silence in the first session, Roberta says, "I don't know what to talk about." I nod, uttering one of those sounds which only a long analytic practice enables us to make with a particular affective colouring every time (in this case, a confirmation that I have heard and invite the patient to go on), and Roberta starts putting her first characters into the field, characters who, as I shall discover over time, will remain quite constant in the first phase of the analysis. So, she tells me about a fellow student on the Masters course in Economics at Bocconi University, a seductive personality who does everything with the aim of pleasing men, blonde, blue-eyed, plunging necklines, sportscar ... I interject, merely saying, "A kind of Barbie", and at this point my intervention, product of a visual rêverie, leads to another line of thought: "Yes, a real Barbie, and just think, I used to be forbidden to play with Barbies, so it was just as well that my granny once bought me one and allowed me to play with it, even though my mother didn't seem to approve." I say, "Something not really serious, futile." She goes on, "Exactly, I had to study and study, and then publish and publish." At this point (perhaps because of a possible intervention from me) the other possible character enters the scene, one who will be Barbie's real opponent: "Yes, in my house all the admiration went to my grandmother who had nearly won the Nobel Prize, working in the USA with Montalcini, and later on founded a hospital in India, working with Mother Theresa of Calcutta."

It is obvious how the theme of femininity has been set up straightaway, on a sliding superegoistic scale (as well as the possible worlds the analysis will open up) from Barbieland to Mother Theresa.

Between cypresses and tigers

In the first session (as soon as she has lain down) Claudia falls silent, and though she came into the room beaming, the climate darkens, like a cloud covering the sun, as is really happening – meteorologically – in the room.

Since her silence continues, I say to her, "It seems that your new position [on the couch] is making you sad, that the sun has disappeared as we have just seen, and this has cast a shadow over you."

"Yes, because I think there are more sad things to talk about than the other kind" (big sigh), and then she starts telling me, one after the other, about the boyfriends she has had, each of whom has gone on to show dark sides which have led to the relationship being broken off.

I say, "These are all really sad stories."

"Yes, but at least work is going well, although what I didn't tell you in our first conversations is that the main reason I'm here is because of my psychosomatic problems."

"And what are they?"

"I'm allergic to cats and cypresses." I wonder if it's only cats, or other kinds of feline too, and then I think about the cypresses: an allergy to bereavement, and this alarms me more. Claudia goes on, "And I have chronic haemorrhoids which make me bleed" – I silently wonder what it is that must be evacuated and causes bleeding. Tigers? Bereavements? Lacerating emotions? – and she goes on to say, "And lastly I also suffer from dietary intolerances" (so take care with the interpretative diet!).

I say, "And you were afraid it would scare me off if I knew these things, but now that you are officially a resident of the couch, you aren't afraid to tell me."

"That's the word," she goes on, "'afraid' is the right word. As a child I always had nightmares about monsters, where animals with claws and teeth were tearing into me ..." (She continues telling me about things that suggest the relationship between evacuation/possibility of containing lacerating emotions.) Perhaps this does not need much commentary.

Luisa's turbulences

Luisa comes to her first session like a frightened fawn, gentle-looking and very pretty.

She dissolves into tears as soon as she lies down. Like a river in full spate which I find myself trying to dam, she tells me about her separation from two previous boyfriends, in a tone of great pain even now. Then about holidays in the *Kinderheim* in Switzerland, where she felt exiled. Then about a sister with leukaemia, receiving chemotherapy.

The account seems to be entirely centred on separations and abandonments which we could call "protagonists" and key points of the story.

The narrative continues with the story of a turbulent period from her own life, in which she had taken drugs, mixed in promiscuous company, ending up at parties of an orgiastic nature, frequenting gambling joints, and associating with the criminal world that hovers around them.

At this point, it is obvious that Luisa is talking about excitatory and antidepressive defences to which she had (has) resorted in order to save herself from undigested, untransformed proto-emotions connected with "abandonments".

Later she tells how she is starting to have memories of being "molested" and "abused" by her grandfather, who often touched her.

Then she tells me a nightmare she had as a child, in which her mother was killed by machine-gun fire.

The proto-emotions connected with "hyper-contained – ♂♂♂♂ – abandonments not transformed and not contained" because they exceed the capacity to be metabolised, "disturb", "abuse", and "touch" her.

She continues by telling me how, after graduation, she had been hit by a car, and how a few months later, she had had an autoimmune illness which involved an allergy to light. In a lighter tone, she then tells me about a group of girlfriends with whom she has breakfasted for years, like the protagonists of *Sex and the City* and how one of them tends to disappear and yet, when present, she steals food from the others. At this point, it seems clear that there is a "ghost" – we could call it a tiger/fawn – which is allergic to the light, knocks her down (knocks itself down), and is actually an extremely violent ghost that would like to machine-gun everybody.

A ghost which survives by "picking" at other people's food, but now needs to be visible: or rather, all those proto-emotional states born out of "abandonments and separations" constitute proto-contents, hyper-beta elements, which tend to be evacuated, in search of containers and transformation, even though this evacuation happens like "machine-gun fire".

The first session of an analysis is the way in which these proto-emotions are "cast", and in which we attempt to give them a name: the story thus becomes one of a girl in the patient's class, who has had a series of tumours which have produced a series of metastases. She tries to stay close to this girl, who has been admitted to the paediatric oncology department, where the doctors are very humane and highly skilled.

On the one hand, there has been a "transformation into tumour" of the accumulated beta elements, but simultaneously their transformation into dream as they are being narrated.

There is an "abandonoma" or "separoma" waiting for further transformation, and the analysis is the oncology department where it will – perhaps – be possible to treat these aggregates of beta elements (the betalomas of Barale and Ferro, 1992).

After the first unsaturated interpretation – "It's incredible how many things have accumulated and how much you've had to keep inside you" – Luisa starts to speak about the girl's elder brother, who takes good care of her, and about the girl threading coloured beads to make little necklaces. Immediately, a caring figure appears, along with an ability to connect things and to develop plans, session by session.

The first manifestation of the beta aggregates is undifferentiated (abandonment and convex proto-emotions); then the "ghost" of anger becomes clear, and instead of taking on an undifferentiated life (for example, panic attacks), takes a more narratable form: the ghost, the machine-gun, anger ...

A particular clinical situation could be that of a girl with selective mutism (but this could just as easily be an adult!) who therefore "nullifies" the possibility of communicating the "fundamental rule": not that this has to be done with children, but it puts us in contact with "someone who cannot speak and will not be able to for some time": we need only think of patients who for a long time conceal the fact that they are having hallucinations (Ferro, 2003a).

The dishonest patient

At this point, it is worth taking a look at the problem of dishonest patients, about which Madeleine Baranger (1963) has much to tell us.

Every patient, in his own way and during certain periods of the analysis, is led to evade the "fundamental rule", and this is part of the game. Baranger's attention is directed to those situations in which the non-observance of the "fundamental rule" and the means used to evade it are highly serious. In these cases, dishonesty is in play: in the sense of a planned and systematic behaviour which alters the authenticity and interest of the analytic process, even though this happens at varying degrees of conscious awareness.

An example might be those patients who, having received an interpretation, reply that they have known this for a long time. But Baranger is not content to explain the patient's dishonesty as a dissociative phenomenon (*splitting* mechanisms were already at the centre of her attention in those years). Starting with the most obvious aspects of the challenge and insult to the "fundamental rule", she addresses the ambiguous situation expressed by the inauthenticity of the material as a desire on the part of the patient to pervert the analytic situation radically, and to reduce the analyst to impotence. In this old study, there are distinctive illuminations, for example, the observation that the level of consciousness of the deceit does not constitute the distinctive characteristic of the dishonesty, as if the patient were using his right to dissociate, but not really to dissociate.

In Madeleine Baranger's work, the patient's dishonesty, which is so unpleasant for the analyst, becomes a fascinating subject for study, a structure which vanishes constantly, but serves the patient's plan to deceive the analyst and himself, a continual oscillation between good faith and falsehood, in search of an omnipotent triumph over the analyst. Meanwhile, the patient flits like Proteus from one shape to another in order, above all, to evade self-definition.

What seems essential in dishonesty is an internal situation of the ego: a multiplicity of simultaneous, contradictory identifications which have not been laid down as sediments, and which do indeed make the analysand live as, and present himself, as various characters without being able to know who he genuinely is (Baranger, 1963, p. 8).

But why allude to this topic? Because it stands at an important crossroads, that of truth/lie. It is a topic that we know was dear to Bion, in the distinction between K and O, and then to Grotstein in the oscillation between Truth and its various degrees of distortion: and Grotstein performs the brilliantly transgressive act of placing dreams in column 2 of the Grid (Grotstein, 2007).

But what is the antidote? I think it may be the concept of tolerable truth, and being able to look at it (Ferro, et al., 2007). To me, an extraordinary example is that proposed by Ogden (2007) in his "On talking as dreaming", in which patients who cannot tolerate the more classical style of communication are gradually led, without their knowing it, into a situation where they find themselves for the first time (or almost) dreaming with someone. Consider the famous lie of the Bishop (in Victor Hugo's *Les Miserables*): when the police arrest Jean Valjean – who had been housed by the Bishop and then stole all his silverware – the Bishop lies, saying he had given it to Valjean himself: in other words, the diminution of the Superego and the non-criminalisation of behaviour open new and unforeseeable paths. We need to know how to play with lies as well.

The magic filter: contributions from Bion and from field theory

A magic filter capable of broadening the field is the prefacing of narrated material with "I dreamed that ..."; this allows the dream-level of the sessions to develop. The most banal communications can be examples of this: if a patient says, even in one of the first sessions, "I had an argument with my wife because she's always complaining about the fruit they give her, but never has the courage to protest", it is clear that this could be seen from many points of view, from the collateral transference to denial, to repressed aggression, to the avoidance of other, even hotter topics. With the magic filter, it is easy to understand them as a communication in the field in which "someone receives something that is not good from someone else, without having the courage to protest", and this will be capable of being brought to subsequent clarification through – we may suppose – interpretations of or in the transference.

This leads me to say that in the end we should perform those operations which allow the "hot air balloon of the analysis" to take flight progressively towards new and different points of view.

Much psychoanalysis looks back, to what has happened and been repressed or split off: in this sense, it could seem to be scientific research based on clues about facts, as it has long been customary to call it, using the paradigm of Sherlock Holmes and the patient Watson, replacing "Elementary my dear Watson" with the no less famous, "You told me yourself ...", overturning the patient's communication, who sees how he has been attributing meanings which are very often utterly remote from him and which had been found in the book of meanings.

On the other hand, not much psychoanalysis looks to the future: that is, to some new thing that may be given life thanks to analysis, and possible new worlds that will be habitable by a patient who makes use of new tools for thinking. In some ways, if we replace the wagons of the old Westerns with new tools like the *Starship Enterprise* in *Star Trek*, where will the patient be able to go, what will he be able to find, what will he be able to think and desire (and we with him)?

Or indeed, if we replace the psychoanalysis of contents (split off or repressed, but, in any case, already given) with a psychoanalysis of the development of "tools" for dreaming/thinking/feeling what will happen. In other words, if we focus on the development of the patient's creativity, what will he find/invent for himself?

We can imagine this point of view as that of someone who had been obliged to see "the same film over and over again" (the old compulsion to repeat) and who unexpectedly found himself, or had been helped to discover himself, in a "multiplex". It is true that he had indeed sometimes felt some interference, heard noises from what he had not known were adjacent screens, but to be able to pass from one to the other to see films never imagined before is no small thing.

Perhaps, better still, we could say that the patient will discover his own status as director, and will learn not to dream the repressed or the split off, but to create – by means of the dreams he will know how to have, starting with the transformation into images of every present or past form of sensoriality – a new unconscious in perpetual expansion, which will be a depository with ever broader boundaries, of memories, fantasies, and film clips. An analysis which looks to the future is not so much a detective story as a spy film or science fiction: that is, of the kind in which we know what could happen if we don't intervene. From this perspective, the analysis is something which should prepare the patient to face the future.

What will happen to a psychosomatic patient? To an obsessional patient? Or to a patient with hallucinations? We are called on to prevent the "foreseeable" happening and to set in motion a new and unforeseeable narrative.

A further step has been taken by those authors who, following Bion, have conceptualised that the development of the capacity to dream is the way to develop the possibility of access to previously unthinkable futures. Ogden (2007, 2009), Grotstein (2007; 2009), and I myself (Ferro, 2008; 2009) have variously developed this line of thought.

Thinking about those films which concern an imminent catastrophe for the human race – what shall we say? an asteroid that could have a devastating impact – we could compare this asteroid to a "lyophilised (or compressed) mass of proto-sensoriality, proto-emotions" which, if not transformed by the patient's dream, or the analyst's (or the field's), will have a devastating impact on the patient's psychic life. We would have symptom-driven stories with symptoms on the psychiatric scale, or stories in which the symptom will be expressed through the ankylosis of the story, which will take the kind of shape that is consequent upon letting life become a symptom. Be that as it may, the "symptom" occurs as the precipitate of "dreams" which it has not been possible to have.

The avoidance of catastrophe, "civil protection", the opening up of new worlds, the arrival in parallel universes will become the new metaphors for the development of the mind. Of course, there is an "upstream", or a "before", but investigating that is certainly not the way to a change of destiny.

Bion leads us to the subjectivation of O: in other words, analytic work is not a question of facts, memories, repressions and resistances, but consists in the subjective way in which each individual transforms Ultimate Reality, the Fact, into alpha elements, into pictograms, into figurations that will enable both memory and forgetting; and this is thanks to the development of the tools that do this work. The film of analysis is precisely the development of these tools which allow us to transform and dream experiences never before sufficiently dreamed. Ogden (2009) says that analysis and the analyst need to dream those dreams which the patient has not been able to dream on his own, and which have become symptoms.

The analytic field, from being a strong concept in which it was the explicit interpretative activity of the analyst on the blind spot/fortress formed by the mutual projective identifications of analyst and patient, has become a potential field in perpetual expansion where all the possible worlds activated by the analytic encounter can acquire substance. What used to belong to one subject or another now belongs to the field: we can therefore think in terms of the field's alpha function, the field's beta elements or proto-emotional turbulences, the field's affective hologram-characters, and the field's transformative and interpretative activity.

The singularity of one or other voice dwindles, and what comes to life is this structure which precedes and permits narrative transformations.

The most significant transformations will be the development and increase (sometimes the constitution) of the tools for thinking.

Recently, Roberto Basile and I wrote, "The analytic field is inhabited by innumerable real and virtual presences in the process of aggregation, and a valid comparison might be with the universe as it is understood today" (Basile and Ferro, 2009, p. 5).

In fact, the analytic field coincides with that unrepeatable "universe" which comes to life at the start of every session, before being temporarily suspended at the end of every session.

The field is inhabited by central characters whom we could call the protagonists, then by the secondary actors, and then the walk-ons; all of these presences can change their roles constantly.

But the human (or not anthropomorphic) character represents the most highly evolved part of the field. We could compare it to the constellations that we are able to make out in a starry sky. The field is the site of an infinity of other phenomena, the majority of which are unknown. An axiom of the field could be that the "big bang" and the "big crash" happen at the beginning and end of every session.

The characters are the destinations of work done "upstream", of which they are the outcome.

The status of the characters is complex and they do not correspond to those people with whom they maintain a superficial resemblance. The characters in the session are the fruit of mental operations carried out by analyst and patient, whose mental functioning (and proto-emotions, emotions, and unknown aspects) they delineate. That is, they are holograms of the mental functioning of the analytic pair, though they also include functioning that, in other kinds of discourse, we would call split off or not yet accessible to thinkability. The characters enter the session at a tangent, and leave it at a tangent, while others who entered tangentially become protagonists, and yet others suddenly take on essential roles.

From this vertex, whatever the patient says describes a functioning of the field.

The analyst's position in it is distinctive: it oscillates between a position of maximum asymmetry (he has the responsibility) and one of maximum symmetry (the functioning of the field is co-determined by analyst and patient).

Conclusion

I believe that the "fundamental rule" could be that of dreaming sensoriality in such a way as to be ever more in contact with the unconscious, which we continually broaden in order to communicate it, and which must be a co-constructed destination experienced more and more session by session with our modes of functioning, and with those of the patient and of the field that we make knowable with him only in *après-coup*.

Let's imagine that after the communication of the classical "fundamental rule", patient A might say, "I'm always relieved when my wife gives me a shopping list", while patient B might instead say, "I can't stand the way my wife always tells what I'm supposed to buy". Who is right?

Neither, obviously, but all the same it is a step on the way to that relative, tolerable knowledge of Pirandello's "Right you are, if you think so".

2

DENIAL, NEGATIVE CAPABILITIES AND CREATIVITY

Introduction

Freud (1925) states that in denial we have an intellectual version of repression, which preserves the essential character of repression, or at least its emotional counterpart. Naturally, we have even stronger defence mechanisms than denial, such as splitting (Dr. Jekyll and Mr. Hyde) or hyperbole, well described by Bion (1965), in which the affect is violently expelled and lost "in space".

It goes without saying that the other side of denial is assertion, which derives from an interpretative activity of the analyst's, or of the patient himself.

In this chapter I will consider these defence mechanisms as points on a sliding scale of the same phenomenon. This is not because I think there is no value in emphasising the differences between them, or their specific character, or even their differing degrees of severity, but because I think it is more useful to offer a reflection on a common antidote to these defence mechanisms: the analyst's negative capabilities as they are understood by Bion (1962) when he picks up this concept from Keats's letter of 1817 to his brothers. The key point of these capabilities is to be able to remain in a state of doubt without having to saturate it instantly with answers, being in "uncertainties, mysteries, doubts, without any irritable reaching after fact and reason:" that is, in Bion's jargon, to be able to stay for a long time in PS (the paranoid-schizoid position), but in a PS without persecution.

It's true that, in doing this, I am assigning fixed roles, but it is purely for convenience; if we think that a field is established between analyst and patient, as the Barangers teach us (Baranger and Baranger, 1961–1962; Ferro and Basile, 2009), then the opposite situation is not infrequent: one in which it may be the analyst who puts up defences against authentically listening to the patient, doing so by means of those interpretations which Bion placed in column 2 of the Grid (that of lies) in order to save himself from an excess of anxiety, and that it may be the patient who perseveres in offering an emotional truth.

From the intrapsychic point of view, I would see denial as a "dyke" which prevents flooding downstream: whatever cannot be metabolised and transformed, the irruption of which would be ruinous to the psychic apparatus, is "denied".

A literary example to which I shall refer only because it is very well known is Melville's story, *Bartleby the Scrivener*, in which the protagonist, who is constantly asked to leave his place of work, politely and firmly replies, "I would prefer not to", in the misguided hope that he will be shielded from the catastrophic experiences which leaving would have caused him.

A look at the relational dimension

There has been much discussion of how to work with the patient who uses denial to withdraw from the interpretation. I have previously recalled (Ferro, 1992) how Freud was sometimes insensitive to the response given to an interpretation: there is an amusing episode in the case study of *The Rat Man* in which he almost forces the patient to accept a reconstruction of his childhood without realising how the patient's association-response denies his intervention. Indeed, straight after Freud's imperious reconstruction (1909), the patient speaks about a professor of law who asked about domiciled bills of exchange.

This problem arises especially with narcissistic patients, and in connection with this, I would like to recall the well-known story of the boy, youngest child of a very poor family, who is the first to go to school because the parents, with the help of the other siblings, are finally able to afford it. Everyone immediately foresees a brilliant future which will free the whole family from their poverty, but on the third day of school the boy says, "I'm not going to school any more", throwing the family into despair. Seeing that their threats and promises are in vain, the parents give up, but ask at least to know the reason why. The boy's reply is, "Because at school they teach me things I don't know."

Naturally, the panorama is changed by the Barangers' field theory, by a non-Kleinian reading of Bion, where Bion (1987) says, for example, that an interpretation will have to be given "six days, six months or six years after it's been thought," and that it would be senseless to launch into explanations of the digestive tract with a new-born infant.

Widlöcher's (1996) concept of co-thinking and the ideas about what in Italy have been called "weak", "unsaturated" or "narrative interpretations" (Ferro, 2002a; 2004) also point in this direction.

This digression is intended to underline how often, the more assertive an interpretation is, the more it activates a denial and sometimes fosters or strengthens a splitting. Going down this route easily leads the work into an impasse, and into negative therapeutic reactions.

Play and negative capabilities as an antidote to denial

I think the best antidote to denial is to create some climatic-affective coordinates, in my dialect *a field*, in which there is a sort of extraterritoriality, where the level of truth/falsehood is lowered in relation to the idea that there is a holder of truth, so that in a sort of duty-free zone it may be possible to generate shared narratives which gradually render the unthinkable thinkable. Besides, the approach to O can only be gradual and must take account of the degree of emotional truth that is tolerable for the patient and for the analyst. Incidentally, I recall that Grotstein (2007) goes so far as to place dreams in column 2 as mediators between Truth and the necessity of masking the absolute unknowable truth.

This is more or less Winnicott's discussion (1971) of analysis as transitional space, the area of interpretations that I would call unsaturated, quite unlike interpretations which engulf and become agents of persecution (Tuckett, et al., 2008).

We can observe how sometimes this type of operation fails, sometimes succeeds, but what matters is that there should be an oscillatory movement between these two dimensions, between the more open and unsaturated, and the other in which an exhaustive interpretation is sought, not always with success.

In Italy, the consideration of what a patient says after an interpretation as a *response* to the interpretation is especially due to Luciana Nissim Momigliano (2001), with the contributions of Haydée Faimberg (1996) on the subject remaining important, but before them Ferenczi (1912) had intuited this aspect of the patient's communication, describing it in his extraordinary paper, "Transitory Symptom-Constructions During the Analysis".

I would like to return to the "negative capabilities": they allow us that particular type of receptivity and unsaturatedness which enables anxieties, sensoriality, and projective identifications to find a sort of "void" which permits both a full reception and a collapse of "truths" that are intolerable to thought. I would say that negative capability is, in this sense, the precursor of every rêverie. The technical tools it draws on are our means of tolerating the difference in significance to analyst and patient which can often arise because of the unsaturatedness of the interpretative interventions.

I believe there is much to be gained from replacing exhaustive interpretation with an inclination towards narrative transformations that can be activated by the analyst's enzymatic interventions.

Furthermore, the way in which we use the patient as our GPS system becomes central: we can take the patient's responses as instructions that he gives us so that we can reach him on an ever-deeper level. Bion (1983) often speaks of the patient as our "best colleague", and for my part I often think of that beautiful story by Conrad, *The Secret Sharer*, in which there is a stowaway on a ship, who is tolerated for a long time by the captain and who, when the ship is near the coast, dives overboard, recognising that the ship is about to run aground against a rock. He waves his hat above the water to signal the presence of the rock, thus enabling the captain to avoid shipwreck. I think this function of the patient, moment by moment waving his hat to tell us how we are progressing, is fundamental. In the end, this is the only way we have of really being in contact with the patient – and I insist on the concept of unison – rather than in contact with our theories, because otherwise we end up in a kind of primal scene with the theories, excluding the patient.

So, we see an emotional field in which there is an oscillation between denial, negation and negative capabilities, which at a fundamental level modulate and regulate the emotional forces which can enter the field and be metabolised.

In this connection, it is also interesting to think back to Bion suggesting that even dreams and waking dreams (alpha function) are to be considered barriers and gaps, compared to a reality (O) that remains unattainable.

I believe that a dialectic between defences and O (the K ↔ O oscillation) remains the best method for approaching truths without being burned by them.

After passing through "denial" and "negative capabilities" (which, let's remember, can also derive from the analyst when he makes the kind of interpretations that would be possible in the second column of the Grid – that is, the row column of lies – blocking the activation of emotions and affects that he fears, or in my dialect, give more space to "grasping" than to "casting") we arrive at the third point: the work of creativity.

The interpretative line

It is not unusual to find oneself caught up in an interpretative line which organises all one's listening (or non-listening).

With Filippo, having in mind the opportunity for him to integrate some violent aspects of himself, I had chosen this wavelength and gone on autopilot, even seeing "big bullies" in the "bolts" of wheels,[1] until one day Filippo tells me about his dentist, who keeps taking X-rays of the same tooth without asking himself if the severe pain might originate in other teeth. A blood test reveals a high percentage of anomalous red corpuscles, but Filippo, consults a second laboratory where doubt is cast on the procedures by which "this analysis" was made.

At this point, I cannot fail to notice how my insistence on one interpretative line may have taken me completely off track.

The interpretative line involves a failure to listen to the new things the patient tells us every day: indeed, we cannot ignore Bion (1987) when he tells us that the patient who finishes a sentence is not the same one who began it. "Listen without memory and desire" also means not being weighed down by preconceptions about the patient and about the interpretative line because these preconceptions obstruct the developments of the field in an original and creative direction.

Isotta and her boyfriend

Isotta is in her first year of analysis. Coming to a session one Monday she offers the following picture: a patient has fled from the community where he is required to stay; then her orphan cousin, who had been more or less adopted by the family, had a series of furious outbursts which resulted in his kicking the door down; her mother broke down in tears at her nephew's wildness, and when her husband came hope, she was angry with him for his lack of involvement in bringing up the children, and dragged up some old recriminations.

Here we encounter the problem of how to cook these varied ingredients: as code-breaking, it would be easy; over the weekend the analyst has moved, gone away, and the rage is uncontainable, leading to kicks being aimed at the closed door and to recriminations at this abandonment.

This interpretation would have two limits: it would be the product of a single mind and would seem automatic, saturated, endowed with one meaning only, and given by an analyst-conjurer who knows and understands everything. The alternative would be to work with the characters and their relationships, foregrounding the emotions between them.

However, this could turn out to be too general. So, the method is to make a start on the second mode and to try out the patient's responses so as to be guided by them in taking the session forward according to what can be "hinted" and what can be said "clearly and explicitly".

The same problem had been posed when Isotta had spoken of her boyfriend who was an "old grump" and wouldn't accept friends' invitations to dinner. In one session, she had spoken about the difficulties of coping with her "grumpy boyfriend", about the disappointments and frustration he caused her, but also saying that she could see his point of view, his difficulty in being with other people. At the end of the session I feel unsatisfied. I seem neither to have caught nor conveyed the "fresh juice of emotional meaning".

Isotta begins the next session by saying, "The bulb in my bedroom blew yesterday and I was left in the dark." This notification (that the session had not provided any light) authorises me, albeit delicately and gradually, to show Isotta how being a grump can also be one of her own more obscure aspects, concealed by her easy-going way of functioning, and that perhaps her talkativeness actually serves to construct a barrier to protect the grump. When Isotta tells me about the good film she has enjoyed seeing, I can add a further meaning: that, on the one hand, coming to analysis is something she likes and does willingly, but on the other, she has difficulty in revealing herself. At this point, she recalls how much she enjoyed dancing as a child, but how embarrassed she was when her family saw her doing it.

What I'm getting at is that there is no right or wrong way of interpreting, but that it must be constantly modulated according to the invaluable directions coming from the patient.

The analyst's function also seems to be that of dreaming the missing pieces until the patient's dream can be developed. It doesn't matter what the dream is, it just needs to develop. This example leads us to reflect on how every communication, even those that seem most real, can be considered as emotional reality, and how every communication from the patient can be considered and heard as "a narrative derivative" of his waking dream-thought, as long as we dare to listen from the vertex of transformation in dream. This permits a completely different kind of listening. The difficulty of this operation is all the greater the more that (apparently) real situations, considered to be external, obstruct the analyst's receptive-dreaming ability, who could thus get lost in the byways of listening like a social worker, a family clinic, a support psychotherapist, abandoning the analytic vertex.

The opposite risk is equally possible, that of an interpretation like a simultaneous translation which strips a story of its emotional intensity, rendering it an intellectualised decoding without affect. The outcome is the necessity to interpret and comprehend in our mind until it becomes possible to extend the field of meaning, myth, and passion (Bion, 1963). In other words, the interpretation must address something which the patient can at least partly see (to pull the rabbit out of the hat, the patient must at least be able to see its ears), the narrative must be warm and made on the spur of the moment, and the same holds about having the characteristic of shared visibility on a narrative-visual-mythic axis.

I postulate as a therapeutic factor the quality of the analyst's mental functioning in the session, and in particular his gifts of receptivity, elasticity, capacity for transformation, tolerance and patience.

These gifts, entering the field, operate transformations that were not previously thinkable: thus, the beta elements – proto-mental, emotional or sensory contents – not previously transformed into pictograms (alpha elements) or not containable, can no longer be "camouflaged", "shelved", split, projected or evacuated, but can have access to thinkability. In the cases described, I have tried to show how the quality of the analyst's mental functioning in the session is a variable of the analytic field and contributes to co-determining it, just as the interpretative choices in a broad sense co-determine the opening or closing of possible worlds.

I think our knowledge is more like a Swiss cheese, full of holes. It's just that we are ashamed and afraid to show how many holes we have, so we spend a great deal of time creating *trompe-l'oeil* to fill – or to pretend, or convince (ourselves), that we have filled – these holes.

Religions, ideologies and fanaticisms are some of the main "fillers" we use. The same goes for the use of theories in the session. This is how we fool ourselves into thinking that we look like a high-density Parmesan and not a trabeculated Emmental. In *Attention and Interpretation*, Bion (1970) writes a few lines about the need for lying, which modestly suggest to us that we can do no more than be tolerant with ourselves and others, giving up being "paladins" of Truth, and enjoying being artisans on the level of developing what is mentally tolerable for our patients and ourselves.

Bion had made a paradoxical eulogy of lying, not only because the lie presupposes a thinker, but above all because what counts is the truth that is tolerable to our thought. This is true for the patient's defences, but at the same time for the defences which the analyst puts into play so as not to succumb to anxiety.

Laura's cut glass

Laura dreams that she is going backwards up a skyscraper, and then that she is in a regal palace full of shawls and fine cut glass; but there is a housekeeper vacuum cleaning and a girl giving herself a beauty treatment (far from romantically) with some slices of cucumber. There was a set of iron shelves on which to replace a large quantity of Barbie-related objects scattered on the floor. The descent from idealisation is a long one; taking the cucumber slices from one's eyes to see the reality of life isn't easy, but a housekeeper is at work tidying up, and there is an iron structure which will permit the make-believe world of childhood to be put away.

Perhaps it would be an effective antidote to an excess of lying to make the transformations in dream that I have described (Ferro, 2009) and which open us to play, to narrative, to creativity:

If, in presenting a clinical case, the analyst dwells on the "hernia" effect which a little boy has suffered following an operation to cure phimosis, and if the symptom of this is mutism, it is not difficult to "dream" the communication in terms of the boy alternating material of incontinence (hernia) with that of hyper-continence (phimosis), and that the mutism can only exist in relation to screaming.

Deconstructing the narrative and dreaming it in the *hic et nunc* is the specific task of the analyst, an analyst who is not too scared to do so. On the whole, however, he is, and he grabs hold of theories like a lost child grabbing his mother. Among its many diseases (symptomatic of its anxiety), the human animal has that of compulsively giving meaning, of finding (often of attributing) a meaning to things that do not have it. But this machine which creates sense and meaning can turn out to be useful for us if we know how to manage it and be conscious of it.

Hume alerted us to the fact that *post hoc* is not necessarily *propter hoc*, so we do not have certainties of any kind, and must always perform from the script.

We know very little about autism, either as a high-profile pathology or as those nuclei or modes of functioning that we all have, and yet we saturate what we cannot tolerate not knowing with stoppers to "plug" the gaps in our knowledge; it is as if we could float using only sense and meaning to buoy us up, but were not able to hover in non-sense or waiting for a meaning, the way certain figures by Chagall do.

The young patient I spoke about earlier makes the stylised drawing of a child, then draws the same child behind some vertical lines. He is rigid, and does not speak: here is the phimosis; "The gorilla is in prison behind these bars". Over time he has crises of violence and screaming, during which he smashes everything. Then he makes a drawing with vertical lines and a frame: the little gorilla has simply escaped from his cage, and the incontinence explodes. In the presentation of the case the analyst had spoken about a cold mother, and then about the fact that the boy had caught chicken pox which had raised his temperature to 41 degrees.

The father is a computer technician who bursts out sobbing in one session.

Here are two other ways of recounting the double mode of functioning: the penguin with the cold mother at the South Pole, and the torrid heat of the 41 degrees. The father who "makes things technical", miniaturises every emotion and is then incontinent with his tears.

The problem is that of finding a balance between a container that explodes and a claustrum that locks up: that is, of finding a container elastic enough to do just that, contain.

An extension of the concept of rêverie to the whole way in which the session is listened to (as a dream, in other words) leads to the concept of transformation in dream.

What the patient narrates is deconstructed in relation to every aspect of external and factual reality, and is considered as a rendering explicit of his dream-thought: that is, as a *narrative derived from it*. This narrative derivative will be referred back to its oneiric matrix.

When a patient talks about his violent brother, her fragile sister, his incontinent grandmother or a biting dog, all these characters must be understood as functions of the field, and the analyst should be able to perform an oneiric transformation of what is being communicated: in other words, the creativity of the field is also a function of our degree of freedom and courage.

Verbal squiggling

Jay Greenberg (2012) coined the expression "verbal squiggling" alluding both to Winnicott's "squiggle" game and to the "field" concept which is becoming ever more widely disseminated: just as analyst and patient take turns in giving meaning to the scribbles made by the other on a piece of paper, so analyst and patient complete the sound scribbles suggested by the other in the co-construction of the co-narration that they make continuously (Stern, 2013; Ferro, 2006b). The phenomena of casting enrich the (co-created) verbal squiggles of patient and analyst, and continuously give form and name to the characters of the sessions.

Characters who, beyond a realist vertex, can be seen from a vertex which views them as internal objects, as the analytic pair's neo-creations to express what comes to life in the field and which will be able at a certain point to take on meaning.

A very serious and committed young neurologist suddenly starts inveighing against psychologists – specifically, the women she works with in the motor rehabilitation department. She is feeling intense rage, rivalry, scorn, jealousy. Not a day goes by without her time being wasted by the psychologists with whom she works closely. We agree – in the film we are co-producing – that she feels the psychologists are "sluts, slags, flirts". But here's the mystery: these are "gifts" which the patient has never had and would like to make her own. Unexpectedly, she changes her point of view and decides to spend more time with the other women, and this is the only way she will succeed in making her own those aspects of her own femininity which had so long remained imprisoned and not been expressed.

Greenberg (2012) has stated that going into the consulting room thinking about Oedipus, would be like reading a murder mystery when you know who did it. And in any case, we know it was always the butler.

We come across this type of analysis very often, made with a pre-determined map and no risk; and Renato Sigurtà, a historic figure in Italian psychoanalysis, used to say that training analyses – precisely because of their pre-determined objective – could be thought of as analyses with a parachute.

This also explains why I have done so few training analyses – which would, after all, be the same as the others (except for the fact that they are conducted by a supposedly more expert analyst) – trying nonetheless to make them as much like the others as possible, and with the same goals, as Bion made so clear in the *Tavistock Seminars* (2005) and at the 1978 conference in Paris, organised by Salomon Resnik. An analyst's consulting room, claims Bion, should be like an artist's studio which, out of chaos, gives life to new creations in an unforeseeable way.

Transformations in play

I have previously expounded at length the concept of transformation in dreaming (Ferro, 2009) and the usefulness of regarding the analytic session as a dream produced together by analyst and patient.

I would like to focus now on another point, or rather the same point in different terminology: that is, on how transformation can also be effected in play, both in the analysis of children and of adults – in the case of the latter, using a more verbal mode in the imaginary theatre of the session.

An experienced colleague finds herself working with a boy who, ever more furious and uncontained, makes little paper rockets and throws them at the analyst. No reasoned interpretation has any effect. So, the analyst decides to join in the game, making little paper rockets and throwing them at the boy, trying to give verbal sense to what is happening. It happens that one of these little rockets hits her in the eye, causing her such pain that she is herself gripped by a blind fury, deliberately throwing a rocket of her own into the boy's eye and hitting it. He is untroubled by this and continues the battle, accompanying it with a stream of the worst swearwords he knows. The analyst is astonished and disoriented by her own action; naturally mortified, she tries to put into words what is happening in the room, but this achieves nothing but a worsening of the boy's rage and a further storm of insults.

Here the analyst has a stroke of genius and transforms the swarm of swearwords into rhyming verses. These verses turn all the boy's swearwords into poetry. This calms the boy, who seems amazed by the unexpected turn which the session has taken and fascinated by the new game.

In the next session, the boy wants to resume the game, telling the analyst to say some swearwords, which this time he will put together into rhyming poetry with meaning: and so a kind of verbal tennis, or rather basketball, is created in which each receives the other's word and transforms it into poetic invective, as was the case in certain verbal games from the Middle Ages.

What had merely been evacuated has become a shared game giving sense to what could previously only expressed physically through movement. In the end, the same type of transformation in play can occur with an adult patient, although with different expressive modalities.

Operations upstream of interpretation

It is not unusual to find ourselves with patients who flood the session with words. They cannot be stopped, in my opinion, although it is sometimes suggested otherwise, because they are affected by a sort of psychic diarrhoea.

It is as if they found themselves with all the words of *War and Peace* inside them (and sometimes this quantity of words is already an achievement in itself) so the analyst has to distil or summarise this evacuation so as to shed light on its main points, characters and functions.

Only at this point will an overview from above enable the organising lines of the field to be read.

In a supervision I once called these "helicopter interpretations", because they try to give a general idea of the troop movements that are necessary before more localised sectors of what is happening in the field can be put under examination.

This same type of operation is often performed in those periods when a patient is not ready to undertake an analysis, and must be guided towards the possibility of it. Some people call this period, which can last a long time, pre-analytic psychotherapy, but I would be more inclined to consider it a necessary preliminary which leads – often painlessly – to the possibility of having an analysis, even when starting from a long way off.

Negative capabilities and creativity in the session

The terrain on which I feel most competent to make a contribution of my own about creativity is naturally that of the analytic situation and what happens in it. Besides, I believe that in this area the problem of creativity concerns us quite specifically. I believe moreover, that this is articulated and presented in different modalities in different models: from the topic of sublimation to that of the long journey towards the depressive position; from the topic of reparation to that of catastrophic change and the reaching of O – or vice versa, the passage from O – along row 2 of the grid towards alpha, its sequences and their narrative derivatives (Ferro, 2010).

I would like to pose myself the problem of when a session can be called creative: I think it is simply when something new arises in it, when it leads to fertility on the part of the analytic pair.

Before moving on to the clinical illustrations I shall use as ways of sharing a sometimes complex theory – like the one I would call "post-Bionian field theory" – some theoretical explanation is necessary, however.

I will speak in dual terms of analyst and patient where the whole would have to be re-thought in terms of the field (Ferro and Basile, 2009) or as Ogden (1994) sees it, the "analytic third": that is, a new, third structure which comes to life in the minds of analyst and patient, but I shall leave this highly complex task to the reader who might want to re-think what I am saying in terms of the field.

There are many "places" where creative processes are carried out: the most significant is the work that leads the analyst's mind to the transformation from sensoriality (beta elements) towards the formation of waking dream-thought: in other words, a sequence of pictograms (constituted from alpha elements) that constitute that skin of thought which originates the contact barrier (Bion, 1962) and to what Bion (1992) called "alpha dream", images that are not directly knowable except within the operations of rêverie, in visual flashes and in night dreams that are a re-dreaming (or at least a sort of montage) of all the alpha elements (pictograms) constructed and stored up while awake. The sequence of images that thus comes to be formed in some way placates, pacifies the mind every time this transformation is achieved.

These pictograms are normally unknowable in themselves. If, for example, we have a sequence of strong, indistinct sensoriality which could be organised by the alpha function into states of rage – relief – nostalgia, then a possible sequence of pictograms could be as follows: Storm – Sun breaking through clouds – Autumn sunset.

Naturally, the choice and construction of the "pictogram" and its sequences are *extremely subjective*. It is as if a "theme" had been painted by Degas, or in turn by Caravaggio, Monet, Chagall, and Picasso. So this is the first "locus" of the mind's creativity. In Bionian jargon it would be the transformation from beta – via alpha function – into alpha.

This is where we find the second site of the mind's creativity: that is, in the likewise *extremely subjective* way in which the sequence of pictograms (waking dream-thought) is "narrated" or put into words through an infinite number of literary genres: now we have reached the narrative derivatives of the pictograms (or of the alpha elements) (Ferro, 2002b; 2006b; 2010).

The proposed sequence could become a series of stories featuring the constant, rage – relief – nostalgia. It goes from a childhood "memory" to a diary account, from a news item to a fantasy, and so on.

It is also true that we can approach a pictogram of the sequence which is formed in our mind in the session by means of that phenomenon called rêverie, by which we enter into contact with, "see" with the mind's eye, the pictogram "storm", for example: it will be for us to find out how to use it in the session.

A brief example: reveries are always oneiric fragments of situations steeped in projective identifications or, if we prefer, beta elements.

With Giovanna, we have reached an impasse, seemingly with no way out, when I come into contact with and *see* "a ship in a bottle" which offers me a visual description of what is happening in the analytic field: the analytic sailing ship has been bottled up, and from this comes the interpretation; it seems to me that we have stalled, like a ship in a bottle, a ship that should be, like the analysis, made for sailing.

It would be a case of metaphor, however, and not of rêverie, if, using my encyclopaedia – that is, my body of knowledge about this subject – I called on an example taken from Conrad; one of those "fair winds" which sailing ships sometimes find themselves riding. This would help me to give a better description of what I already know: that the image of the "ship in a bottle" contributes to, or rather suggests the interpretation, acting as its starting point and inspiration.

In my opinion, there is a big difference between "free associations" and reveries: the latter are characterised by direct contact with an image (which will naturally not be communicable to the patient – or only in exceptional circumstances – and in such a case would turn into self-disclosure).

Free associations occur within what I have called narrative derivatives, whereas reveries are concerned with, I repeat, making direct contact with the pictograms which constitute waking dream-thought.

Another situation where we see a pictogram of the sequence of such waking dream-thought is when the patient projects one of these images outwards without violence and without it being an actual hallucination, because the meaning conveyed by this image is easy to intuit. As an illustration, I recall the patient I have already quoted several times, saying when I asked her for an increased fee, "My God, *I can see* a chicken being plucked on the opposite wall."

But let's go back to explaining the model of the mind to which I am referring: during the day we will have stored up an enormous quantity of pictograms (alpha elements), and this duly requires a "super alpha function" (Grotstein, 2007; Ferro, 2010), a sort of second pressing/weaving of this store until it results in the dream images as thoroughly digested as they can be by our thinking apparatus.

It is no coincidence that Ogden (2009) maintains that the goal and work of psychoanalysis consist in dreaming those dreams, bringing about those transformations from storms of sensoriality into images which the patient is not able to do on his own. The consequence of this is that the goal of analysis is the development of the ability to "generate images", to create dreams where there were symptoms, or concretisations of sensoriality.

The greater success of creativity in psychoanalysis does not so much concern contents as the possibility of developing those tools (alpha function and ♀♂) which are able to augment the ability to dream, think, and feel – that is, the operation described by Grotstein as the ability to subjectify O, and by me (Ferro, 2009) as "transformations in dreaming", which enables the de-concretisation, de-construction, and re-dreaming of all the patient's communications. Let's remember that this should all be re-postulated in terms of the functioning of the analytic field.

Naturally, the "visual" in analysis does not stop here: it would include the enormous chapter of the drawings produced in analysis, not necessarily in child analysis, which, on the analogy of narrative derivatives, we will consider as graphic derivatives of waking dream-thought (Ferro, et al., 2007).

In any case, the fabric of a session is more often than not a dance between narratives of a visual character – reveries, metaphors, dreams – as we can see in the session which follows.

A net for Satan

PATIENT: I've got two dreams today. Shall I "shoot"?

ANALYST: (*in a voice which shows he has noted the "shoot"*) By all means!

PATIENT: In the last one I had a Hummer with four enormous wheels which made it possible to explore other planets, and which worked on all types of terrain. … Then I was on Mars where I could see things never seen before…. Then there was a tunnel and a space that opened out into rooms, but I didn't like the way mother had furnished it. Then yesterday evening at dinner I found my father especially unpleasant, I felt disgusted and thought, *if only he'd die*, but I really thought it, not as a figure of speech; my girlfriend actually said even worse things about my father. (*Here he stops as if waiting for something from me*)

ANALYST: It seems to me that the Hummer, the analysis with the four wheels enables you to see what is happening even on Mars, even from unknown viewpoints. There are things that your Mum does that you don't like. Then your Dad disgusts you, and maybe you wouldn't only like to see him dead, for real, but you'd shoot him, kill him yourself. And then there's what you can't say and your girlfriend says instead – what you have filtered out. It seems as if, from an unknown, Martian point of view, you hate me and would happily kill me, once you've given me a proper earful.

PATIENT: (*He is astonished, fascinated, incredulous and convinced by this communication*) I would never have believed that I could think something like that! (*Long pause, seemingly for amazed reflection*)

ANALYST: But what about the other dream?

PATIENT: Yes, I was in a lecture theatre at a university, being accused of murder by a load of doctors, but I knew I was innocent, and so I was calm. Then these doctors followed me to my uncle Emanuele's house, he's a painter who teaches at Brera, and I liked going there when I was young. The doctors were still after me and then I realised that Satan was beside me yelling terribly at the doctors in a huge voice that terrified me.

ANALYST: What I told you about the fact that you'd like to murder me might imply an accusation, but you know you haven't killed me. The evidence for that is the fact that I'm here talking to you. You also like going to uncle Emanuele's house, you like analysis, but sometimes I insist too much, I make you really angry and then you become Satan yelling at me in a huge voice to make me stop.

PATIENT: (*thoughtful*) Well, I'm now thinking of a recurring dream that I had as a child. I was being pursued, chased by a Tyrannosaurus rex. I was terrified, but this is the first time I've thought about being terrified of my own anger, that the Tyrannosaurus or Satan was me.

A few months later:

PATIENT: I'm glad that Maddalena (*his girlfriend*) is going to be away for two months (*having gained a Master's degree in Economics, which "naturally" coincides with my summer holiday*) I'd like to buy a Labrador.

ANALYST: (*I'm thinking of labbra-d'or* ["golden lips"] – *an affectionate thought, delicate but also compliant.*) I wonder what a "Bouvier des Flandres" would say, seeing himself abandoned at what we know is a very delicate time for him?

PATIENT: (*without a moment's hesitation*) You rotten cow, you whore, how can you leave me at a time like this?

ANALYST: So why do you have to be (*enunciating the phrase clearly*) the *labbra-d'or* who only says affectionate things?

PATIENT: Because it's as if I don't have a fence strong enough to keep in Dobermanns, wolves, or Mastiffs, but it is just about strong enough for Labradors.

ANALYST: (*lightly*) So you need a bit of *ferro* [iron] to strengthen the net. To conclude, I would like to recall that in *Elements* (1963) Bion tells us that interpretation should involve an extension of the *field of passion, sense and myth*.

This claim leads us to develop a metaphor that will accompany the interpretation, which thus becomes composed of a first part and a second with a metaphorical extension, one that turns what had been briefly sketched out into narrative, into image (and these metaphors belong to our own personal encyclopaedia of metaphors).

The first characteristic needed by a metaphor is clarity and relevance to the subject in hand. So, it is an image which arises out of the interpretative context and completes it, being "made to measure", despite coming out of the creative department.

Rêverie is different because it comes into being upstream of interpretation and in a way inspires it, suggests it. Interpretation draws inspiration from it. Rêverie is an image created in the mind (spontaneously and not to commission) and its difficulty consists in how it is to be organised into a relevant, clarifying communication which is not the product of an encyclopaedia (our collection of possible metaphors) but created uniquely and on the spot, almost an excerpt from a dream, definitely a visual pictogram, the outcome of the waking dream-thought that is constantly being produced (ultimately, rêverie is a visual pictogram). The metaphor intervenes in a more developed state, further downstream, when we are still dealing with narrative derivatives. It is an enlarging of narrative that we can use both in clinical practice and in the expounding of theory (Bion, 2005).

The other's mind must be receptive, capable of absorbing, containing and giving the method, and then of transforming proto-sensory and proto-emotional states into images and thence into thought. Things don't always go like that: sometimes we have varying degrees of negative rêverie (–R), from partly or totally obstructed rêverie to extreme situations in which there is an inversion of functioning, and the mind that should accept and transform projects into the mind that wants and needs to evacuate and find space and a method for managing proto-emotions. These mental functions, these traumatic facts (and trauma consists to a great extent in being in the presence of more beta elements than one can accept and transform either alone or with the other's help) are then narrated according to infinite possible scenarios. By which I mean that any narrative, including those that seem most realistic, always tell us something else: that is, they tell us about the patient's inner world and, above all – if we know how to listen – tell us about the adequacy/inadequacy of the tools (for feeling, dreaming, thinking) at our disposal. For me, analysis is to a large extent concerned with all the methods by which these tools (and devices) can be developed (sometimes created).

Note

1   Translator's note: The author plays on "bullo", a bully or hooligan, and "bullone", a bolt.

3

MAKING THE BEST OF A BAD JOB

Research in the consulting room

Premise: what kinds of research exist today in psychoanalysis?

It is generally agreed that there are different types, methodologies and goals of research in psychoanalysis (Frisch, et al., 2010), from the empirical to the conceptual (Leuzinger-Bohleber, et al., 2003).

We have fully scientific approaches in the classical sense, such as the significant and helpful work of Leuzinger-Bohleber, and other approaches pursued for many years in child development research by Fonagy and his colleagues who have opened up new and unsuspected doors to our knowledge and have had an important impact in the psychoanalytic world. Then we have small group research like that being carried out by D. Tuckett, which aims at evaluating what might or might not be comparable in the various forms of psychoanalysis, and this work has led to a multi-authored book edited by Tuckett himself (Tuckett, et al., 2008). The same is true for other work being done in small groups in that laboratory of psychoanalytic research which is the FEP (European Federation of Psychoanalysis), initially coordinated by H. Faimberg and E. Sechaux and others, sometimes with divergent aims but alike in considering "the small group as the site, and at the same time the method, of research".

I would like to offer a reflection on a particular way of doing research that has perhaps fallen out of use and is "unfashionable" in certain psychoanalytic milieux.

We have the privilege of using a constantly funded laboratory in which therapy and research coincide: that is, we have "our poor but invaluable and irreplaceable consulting room". I think this is an indispensable way of doing research in psychoanalysis, and I say this while also being convinced about the usefulness of other methods.

In the analytic situation we do many more things than we realise, and recognising and naming these things is the aim of psychoanalytic research (Di Chiara, 1982).

This research method – the most important in my opinion – has provoked much puzzlement about its scientific status, but I can easily answer that by using the beautiful, intense words of Grotstein (2007) from the closing pages of his *A Beam of Intense Darkness*, which courageously show us the catastrophic change produced by Bion's work which, unlike Freud's – who had sought a scientific consensus – postulates, correctly in my opinion, the need for psychoanalysis to be a different kind of science:

Bion, the intrepid tank commander, took a different direction and attacked science's flank. "Science," he claimed, was appropriate only for inanimate objects. The "science" that is apposite for psychoanalysis is a "mystical science", a science of emotions that are infinite and consequently complex and non-linear in nature. (Grotstein, 2007, p. 328)

I also like to recall another statement by the same author, which sums up Bion's viewpoint: "We become what we agree to suffer" (ibid.).

A little map for finding my way

I also think we can distinguish a metapsychological research of the kind many writers undertake (Green, for example, who uses metapsychology as a sort of "search engine" capable of opening up new conceptualisations; to some degree perhaps, like someone approaching physics by way of mathematics) from the kind that I would call research in the consulting room, which tries to make something new, however minute, burgeon in – and because of – the experience in the consulting room.

Having already plundered Bion in my title, I would just like to recall a few passages:

our rudimentary equipment for 'thinking' thoughts is adequate when the problems are associated with the inanimate, but not when the object for investigation is the phenomenon of life itself. Confronted with the complexities of the human mind the analyst must be circumspect in following even accepted scientific method.

(Bion, 1962, vi, 14)

Bion (1962, xiii, 39) further proposes that we acknowledge "the fact that any session is a new session and therefore an unknown situation that must be psycho-analytically investigated" and that ideally this "is not obscured by an already over-plentiful fund of pre-and misconception". These are not very different from the claims made in his final work, the Tavistock Seminars (2005), product of an interview from June 1976:

I am not very interested in the theories of psychoanalysis; the important point is … the practice of analysis, the practice of treatment, the practice of communication … the evidence I get from my senses while the patient is with me is worth 99, and all the rest share the remaining 1 between them … I think the theory of the conscious and unconscious – which is extremely useful ... becomes a bit of a pest after a time because it gets in the way of being able to see other things that one doesn't know – stands in the way of one's own ignorance.

(pp. 16, 19, 21)

What subjects for research have most intrigued me?

A concept which has fascinated me from the start is how the quality of the analyst's mental functioning on a given day is a factor of development or dysfunction for the patient.

In other words, alongside the central problem of rêverie and "negative capability" (staying in PS without persecution, until the deferrable interpretation can be formulated) I was presented with the problem of negative rêverie (–R) – which I spoke about in one of my earliest papers

(Ferro, 1987): that is, all those situations in which the flow of functioning between patient and analyst is inverted.

I remember that, during the evening when I presented this paper at the Milanese Centre for Psychoanalysis, an old analyst said to me, referring to the supposed dysfunction of the analyst's mind that could pollute the patient's mind, "When you think you've done a bad job, you can be sure that you haven't done a worse one than usual."

Another colleague, perhaps less orthodox and less anchored to what is known, told me that this concept seemed to open a very important path for the future. A third agreed, saying that it was too soon to speak about these things, but that this would be the dominant line of future psychoanalytic research.

Thirty years later it has been universally established that the analyst's mind is not an invariant, and it is a short step from this to an interest in field theories (Ferro, 1992; 1996; 2002b).

A second area of research is the quality to be attributed to the characters who come and go during the analytic hour, and are transformed in it. What status do they have: realistic-historical, internal objects (whether projected or not), or holograms of the couple's mental functioning?

Sometimes, with a certain degree of unease and distress, I re-read some of my old sessions, when I used to work more "by the book" than "with my heart and gut instincts" I also remember a dream recounted by a patient: she was looking out of a window when she was terrified to see an officer from the occupying army in a raincoat, knocking at the door. I had the nerve to interpret this as a persecutory primal scene viewed from inside the womb.

As time went by I asked myself some questions:

a   Do we all agree that an interpretation is subject to confirmation by the patient? Not his "yea" or "nay" but the evaluation of how he responds on a scale from "I received a lovely present yesterday" to "Yesterday they bombed Baghdad."

b   Do we all agree that the "simplicity" of the interpretation is fundamental, albeit with varying degrees of saturation? For example: "Sometimes you feel that somebody is blaming you, and that frightens you" (if formulated in an unsaturated way), or "Sometimes you are frightened by the way I go on at you" if formulated in a more saturated way.

c   Do we all agree that the dream opens up an enormous problem? Must it be decrypted or, since it is the richest communication of alpha elements, must it be intuited as a poem or painting would be, perhaps one by Picasso?

d   Do we all agree that self-disclosure is absolutely bad? It doesn't play a habitual part in my practice, but when I saw that it had become an official tool of American psychoanalysis, I sometimes found myself making use of it, with extreme caution and, I must say, without disturbing the conduct of the session or causing sink-holes to appear in the following sessions.

e   Do we all agree that we never need to answer the patient's questions? For example, "Doctor, do you have a driver's license?" Are we sure that the most correct answer is, "Are you wondering if I'm able to carry out your analysis?" And what if one of us replied on a range from "Why ever wouldn't I have one?" to "We'd really be in trouble if I didn't have one!" (I do, in fact, have the necessary "license" to work as a psychoanalyst!).

Day to day observation in my analytic laboratory of the answers given by my patients has led me to make theoretical-technical changes (with undeniable influences on my technique because of my permeabilization to the psychoanalytic culture with which I was coming into contact).

The key points, which I shall just mention briefly (see Ferro, 2009) are: near-abolition of symbolic interpretations, of the continuous interpretations of the transference (replaced by interpretations in the transference or in the field); the use of unsaturated/narrative interpretations; the varying of the characters in the session as witnesses of the session's varying atmosphere; the development of dream-thinking in the session; the prevalence of the development of tools for thinking, dreaming, feeling, rather than developing the contents of these activities.

How do we position ourselves, so as not to be alone?

The Rosetta Stone

Bion draws our attention to the risk of wrapping ourselves in our theories like warm blankets to protect ourselves from what we do not know. For me, the main thing is to understand the languages and – where possible – even the dialects of the other models and theories because this deepens and broadens my vision.

If a patient were to say, "Last night I dreamed I had to go to the toilet, but I couldn't, I was all blocked up", do I have to believe that the only useful reading will be one related to the patient's desire to tell me things while being unable to say them? Or could there be innumerable other possible "interventions" available to the analyst?

So, this is the kind of problem the small group works on, where we learn to hear the voice of others (and the unconscious is always an Other).

But there is also a kind of research that we can do on our own, about the best way – in our opinion – of intervening, always guided by the GPS which is the patient's unconscious (or the unconscious functioning of the field).

But on venturing into these reflections, we immediately run into a number of problems (Bonaminio, 2003; Borgogno, 2011).

Orthodoxy and science

I was recently at an international conference where I had occasion to listen to a gifted French colleague acting as discussant to another participant's paper, a clearly post-Bionian text which he criticised from a radically Freudian viewpoint, with the same strange effect that a particle physicist would experience if, after speaking about mesons and bosons, he heard himself being criticised for not speaking about levers and fulcrums and their (undeniable) importance and usefulness.

This does not mean that Newtonian physics is less valuable than particle physics. The latter would be no use for building bridges or tunnels, but these are two different matters, as are the various powerful models and theories available to psychoanalysts today (Freudian, Kleinian, Bionian, intersubjectivist, Ego psychology, and so on, along with the whole range of sub-models orbiting each one).

These models are incommensurable: perhaps they can find some common ground as Wallerstein (1988, 1990) rather optimistically wrote, or perhaps we should refer to "clinical thought" as Green (1989, 2005) claimed more recently.

There is no place for orthodoxy in psychoanalysis if it is to be a science, and the 2009 IPA Congress in Chicago focused on precisely this recognition of different models in psychoanalysis. Orthodoxy is a matter for religions. Science is a matter of "facts".

Bion (2005) wrote that we make use of fragments of theories with which we build the theoretical wreckage we cling to – such is our fear of not knowing – but when it encounters a fact this wreckage sinks no less completely than the Titanic did when it met an iceberg.

We are too afraid of the mind and of the unknown not to be constantly tempted to exorcise them by thinking that the paramnesias which compose our theories are true and credible. We know very little about them, and every attempt to know more is often stigmatised as something that infringes a supposed orthodoxy, a supposed "real psychoanalysis".

Nobody could fail to take account of the developments in quantum physics or the introduction of antibiotics for curing infectious diseases: nor should they in psychoanalysis, where we have too long allowed ourselves the luxury of ignoring whatever disturbs what we already know.

So, we have managed to slow down the development of psychoanalysis in an incredible way by making it into a religion. During a seminar, a colleague I hold in high esteem asked a young colleague why on earth her husband, a talented biologist, did not start every paper by quoting Darwin, but only took the most recent work into consideration. She answered that Freud's ideas have not become part of the shared intellectual heritage, and so it was necessary to reaffirm them. I won't conceal the fact that I was left unconvinced by this reply (and still am), and by the necessity for a living psychoanalysis always to start ab ovo or, worse still, from ipse dixit.

Let's remember that what happened to Galileo continues to happen in various psychoanalytic contexts (not everywhere, fortunately) where from time to time we hear the anathema, "This is not psychoanalysis!"

So, the psychoanalytic establishment has perpetrated abuses no different from those of the Church (fortunately without burnings at the stake), whose victims have included Bion (see Grotstein, 2007) and to some extent Meltzer (the former, an absolute genius of psychoanalysis and the latter a really creative analyst).

Many psychoanalytic theorisations – as Bion (2005) constantly recalls – resemble complex delusions that form like scar tissue on the wounds of our not knowing. Every single thing can be explained, given meaning, deduced from a theoretical system which has already foreseen everything. In a child's drawing it will be highly significant if there are three trees or only two! There is a method for deconstructing dreams which will lead us to the dream's real meaning, and so on ...

We really do not know how to live with the holes in our not-knowing. We are like carpenters constantly plugging the hull of a ship, which is actually no more than a thin fabric between the holes.

We keep fitting "patches" to stop ourselves foundering in not-knowing, the not-knowing that terrifies us so that we create "religious systems" as padding against the depressive shipwreck. We actually know very little, and that very little only in an uncertain and provisional way, and yet these systems of psychoanalytic teleology find their way onto university courses. The operation is completed in the session through continual operations of "transformation in hallucinosis" – in other words, we project what we have constructed, thought, or more often learned, onto the patient and then we read this "projection" as being self-evident. It is as if we had sprayed white rabbits with green and blue paint and then authoritatively claimed – as seems obvious – that rabbits are green and blue, and if they aren't green and blue they aren't rabbits.

But why are we so terrified of not knowing? Bion reminds us of this in all his Seminars (1983; 1987; 2005), and I say again, most of our theories (and in the long run all of them, if they are not continually revitalised) are paramnesias that will sink like the Titanic when they run into a fact.

We often work in the same way in the session, always seeing what we know (or think we know): if medicine had worked like this we would still be in the world of "black bile" and the self-evident necessity of enemas and bloodletting, the world of Molière's *Malade imaginaire*.

It costs us a lot to be a species with no before or after, to be only a small step between other befores and other possible afters: a species in transition. A species with no meaning other than to be a suffering and absurd joke of nature, as Lucretius put it.

Faith in something is so necessary for the cementing of an identity that, in one way or another, anyone who instils doubts is burned at the stake or, in this more democratic epoch, simply expelled. What is more, it is incredible that concepts like Bion's "waking dream-thought" or those expressed in Ogden's "On talking-as-dreaming" can be ignored despite the theoretical and technical revolution they imply (in medicine it would be like still using anti-typhoid serum instead of antibiotics).

Now we are getting close to the clinical material that will provide us with a more open way of theorising, so let's start from my point "a" above.

The analyst's mind is not an invariant of the field

Because every day goes differently, because the analyst's alpha function and his "apparatus for thinking thoughts" do not only have to grapple with what "comes from" the patient, and so the depth of the availability of the analyst's mind can vary (though if the analyst's own personal analysis was good enough, this should permit him to sustain a generally well-functioning regime) depending on what comes to him from other emotionally significant situations.

Because what comes from the patient can exceed the analyst's capacity to take it on and transform it, leaving him to a varying extent clogged up. This is all part of the rules of the psychoanalytic game.

Because every patient – and each patient's varied material – has a different impact on the analyst's mind since it strikes differently on his constellations of anxieties and defences.

So, if the analyst is not a neutral tool, but co-determines what happens in the field, what characteristics should he have?

A young colleague in training amazed me with a question about what fundamental gifts an analyst should have. I didn't give him a theoretical answer (I could have cited dozens of texts on the subject) but one off the cuff: benevolence, trust in his method, the ability to blind himself to any reality that is not that of the consulting room.

Benevolence means getting into contact with the feeling that even the most "horrible" of patients matches a similar, often unintegrated, lump within us. There is no patient who does not speak to us about our own remote and often silent wastelands. Benevolence means both the capacity for goodwill and, even more, to view the world like Manzoni's Brother Cristoforo, *omnia munda mundis*: or better still, like the Bishop in Les Miserables, mentioned earlier.

Trust means faith in the fact that the method works, that it will take months or years, but in the end we will have succeeded in doing something helpful with even the most terrible of patients, holding fast to something we know: "that analysis works" because we have experienced it in ourselves.

And third, blindness to all external reality allows us to see scenes in the consulting room that the glare of external reality would obliterate.

In one session we are the "Russian call-girls" who save the patient from depression; in another, "my monster of a husband who's the absolute limit, expecting me to make love when I'm completely worn out" (this after a transference interpretation): but we are also "the scalding hot water bottle", "the cousin who keeps rejecting me, even though all I do is think of her[1] day and night", "the dog that bit me", and so on.

There are no external scenes if we make it dark all around us: the dramatization of the analytic scene takes on density, life and body, and so we can have a truly transformative function within it. We can tune in to the "jealous wife", to the "pain of being rejected". In short, the consulting room becomes the stage where the whole of Shakespeare, Pirandello, Molière, Ibsen and the rest come to life in an infinity of affective storylines which lose substance and vitality if we let in the light from outside. I used to say that in a cinema, you need to keep the emergency lights turned on, but it has to be dark. We allow life and light in the consulting room if we make it completely dark outside (Ferruta, 2003).

Of course, this does not mean taking substance away from historical or existential reality, but allowing it to become embodied there, in the only place where it can be transformed, and if "my boyfriend won't answer his phone" to live through the pain of this with the patient, knowing that it is we ourselves who have not answered, and that it would be too simple to interpret it. First, we must "answer".

Thinking about the internal object that does not answer – the mother who has not answered in the past – stops the drama coming fully to life in the consulting room; whereas, if we are aware and the patient is not, we will continue to be called the "boyfriend", and the drama will stay alive.

And if a patient asks what we think of homosexual relationships and tells us about her constant quarrels with her husband, here is our own homosexual relationship with the patient being brought into view, one in which neither listens to the opinions of the other, and we are the same ("homo") in that each is trying to bully the other into listening. We can only see and transform what we think is alive there.

An accident and emergency department admits a patient made ill by poisonous mushrooms or salmonella in seafood or viral hepatitis. What does the doctor do? – he works with the patient, his symptoms, the damage to his organs and provides dialysis, but as a physician he can do nothing to improve the cultivation and harvesting of fungi or seafood.

The same is true for the analyst who finds himself faced with the effects caused by external reality, but with no jurisdiction over them because they are the responsibility of other professionals. That is to say, we have a responsibility to address the effect of "things" but not the things themselves.

It is not always easy to hold this point of view: a gifted analyst tells me that she has found herself treating a patient following a traumatic event. The patient has lost the use of her left eye and has a paresis of the left side of her body. The realistic, traumatic aspect is so much to the fore that the analyst addresses only this. She does not take into account the fact that the patient is finding a way to express the fact that, being an affectionate, good-natured, generous young woman, she has lost contact with her own "left eye" and the "left part of her body has been numbed, as if by curare": in other words, her diabolical (left, sinister) way of seeing and looking has been de-activated and replaced with a neutral prosthesis. So, the diabolical part has been paralysed.

It is not the concrete that concerns us as analysts, but the hidden meaning that comes to life when the patient's communication is conjoined with the dreaming listening of the analyst.

Why do we sometimes look in the past, in external reality, either defensively using methods we consider more scientific, or more innocently clutching at well-known theories or handbooks?

I think it is for one reason only: because we are terrified by our own unconscious, and we can't wait to shift it into any territory but ourselves, because searching in our own laboratory, our own unconscious, puts us in contact with *The Cabinet of Dr Caligari*, with the madness of the lethargic Cesare and the director of the asylum. We would like to answer this request with the famous response, quoted earlier, of Melville's Bartleby the Scrivener, "I would prefer *not* to".

The slowness of change

I have always been struck by the slowness with which new technical tools, models and paradigms are accepted. For example, in surgery, the arrival of a new instrument (the endoscope) will provoke resistance and opposition that soon diminishes if the instrument is genuinely useful. The same holds true for a pharmacist: antibiotics are a classic example, and no physician would dare not to prescribe an antibiotic in a case of serious infectious illness. It isn't like this in psychoanalysis: even projective identification is still understood in extremely different ways, and considered by some to be a non-existent tool; to say nothing of enactment, rêverie, and – the emblematic case – self-disclosure, which is normal practice in vast areas of the analytic culture and demonised in many others. A truly "scientific" standpoint would be to experience it and then judge whether it is useless, harmful, or useful.

But things don't stop here. Bion repeatedly postulated (mostly in Cogitations) the concept of "waking dream-thought", and he himself noted in the Tavistock Seminars that nobody seemed to have taken any notice of this instrument and concept, a situation which persists today even though it is considered by some to be a concept capable of revolutionising the whole of psychoanalytic technique.

Transformation in the analyst's hallucinosis

Another phenomenon at which we are present is that of a violent projection of theory into the patient's material, the meaning of which is then seen as self-evident because of this projection.

Bloody sheets can only refer to the primal scene, a salmon is the penis, a balloon is the breast; all of which leads to the construction of a hyper-saturated encyclopaedia in which almost every meaning is anticipated and codified.

There is a thick booklet which gives a series of amusing possible answers to the same statement by the patient, depending on the theories to which the analyst subscribes.[2]

Why is it difficult for many analysts to acknowledge and take on the negative transference?

The first patient in a series of three seen in rapid succession for consultations, tells me that her analysis has been blocked and then broken off because of a recurrent dream: she was going home when somebody started following her. She walked more quickly towards her house, went in, and closed the door, but the man was able to get in nevertheless. Then she fled to an even more protected part of the house and locked the door, but this time the man blew down the door with a loaded pistol and started firing.

The second patient stops his analysis after a dream which becomes a repetitive obsession: he was attacked by Mafiosi who were part of an international gang. Three of them in particular were trying to kill him with a long knife, stabbing him repeatedly so that he was bleeding all over, until he escaped by jumping out of the window.

The third case is not very different: a sequence of dreams is taking shape around an experience of something persecutory and threatening which progressively takes on the likeness of a lady who becomes more and more menacing, partly mechanical, partly with vampire teeth.... He runs away.

Of course, following classical theory, these dreams should be interpreted by gaining access to their latent meaning, going well beyond their manifest meaning; but if we consider the dream as the communication richest in alpha elements, as the mind's poetry, the persecutory meaning of the analysis and of the analyst's – or rather, ex-analyst's – own technique seems indisputably obvious.

The dream: let's dream another, but sing Mass

We have an official model of dream-interpretation, the Freudian, which we can sum up as arriving at its true latent meaning thanks to the free associations with the dream – helping us to pass behind the dream-work.

The model has changed a lot since this formulation; the associations have been widened to include what the patient says before and after the dream, and even the analyst's thoughts/associations.

The panorama was revolutionised by Meltzer saying that the analyst can do no more than dream the dream the patient has already had. Then Bion introduced a catastrophe with a further model of the mind, in which it is the waking dream-thought – that is, the work of the alpha function – which transforms little storms or whirlwinds of beta elements/sensoriality into affective-visual pictograms, or alpha elements. The totality of these goes to form the nocturnal dream, which is the product of the "montage of these alpha elements through the work of a director", or the product of a re-dreaming by a super alpha function. The dream can only be intuited and captured by the analyst's rêverie when he is capable of it.

In *Cogitations*, dated 27 July 1959, Bion claims

> But Freud meant by dream-work that unconscious material, which would otherwise be perfectly comprehensible, was transformed into a dream, and that the dream-work needed to be undone to make the now incomprehensible dream comprehensible. I mean that the conscious material has to subjected to dream-work to render it fit for storing, selection, and suitable for transformation from paranoid-schizoid position to depressive position, and that unconscious pre-verbal material has to be subjected to reciprocal dream-work for the same purpose.
>
> *(Bion, 1992, p. 43)*

But instead of stimulating and opening up a debate or a comparison, all this has passed into the most complete indifference. It is sometimes the case that the bearers of a fantastical religious power attempt to make it an "orthodoxy": Bion, for example, gave us technical tools and theories that should have entailed an enormous change in technique, and yet nothing has happened.

The phobia about emotional contact: hic et nunc/*other scenarios*

A patient starts her second analysis by saying that before the first session she had dreamed of having oral sex with her analyst and now, at the start of her analysis with me, she is embarrassed and deeply ashamed because she has dreamt of making love with me. I tell her that she seems to be wanting something right from the start, a really intimate relationship with someone: she bursts into tears.

At her first session, another patient tells me about her husband's ferocity; it's like that of the pitbulls they keep at their country house. I tell her that it wouldn't surprise me if there were not a great deal of fragility and pain behind her husband's ferocity. She weeps silently. Then she adds that she vividly remembers when her father had hugged her husband, and he'd told her that the hug had been like the milk the farm workers used to give him when he was a child, fresh from the cow. But how and why were positive characters coming into the picture? – the hugging father, the new milk, etc.

In another case, the analyst tells the patient that there will be a two-week break, and the patient immediately talks about an epileptic boy who has started having fits again. This example – presented in a group – created general astonishment when I asked "the name of the medication the boy was taking". The group talked about everything but the actual name of the medication: that is, iron (Ferro) the analyst's name.

Lying in order to survive

I find myself re-analysing a patient and, to begin with, some characters he had brought to me over the years have been left as dead letters (for convenience, we'll pass over the present significance of the narrative), as if there had been a ban on "fly-posting" which stopped any possible films being advertised; as if some tacit agreement had meant that certain posters had not been approved by the censor.

Speaking at length about an article on compulsive suicide attempts which had not been accepted for publication by a journal (the analyst who had not been willing to come into contact with the patient's suicidal and depressive anxieties?)

Speaking about a "head-on collision" in which the patient had been involved (and the theme of the "head-on collision" was never developed, at least in the Show Down at the OK Corral version).

Speaking about a tenant in the block where his previous analyst worked, a tenant whom he often met and who seemed to be a "depressive", afflicted by an even worse depression than he was himself: this topic was likewise never brought to life in a session.

Neither was space given to a distant kinship with a Sicilian bandit well-known in the Fifties, or to a troublemaking cousin, or to an uncle who was a bit of a crook (and it's true that the patient never received a receipt for tax purposes from the first analyst!), or another uncle with autistic features.

I mean that that the analyst often acts as a great anaesthetist or stifler of "possible stories" whose subversive power is often left *in nuce*, in favour of more normopathic, "suitable" or orthodox features.

Maybe orthodoxy (and hence an adaptation to the known and the shared) is involved in all this as a phobia of possible subversions, and whereas psychoanalysis had an incredible subversive power, many people now call on it instead to smooth things over with the maps of a pseudo-normality.

But this is not psychoanalysis

You can't interpret a dream without associations.

Elena and the emotions

Elena has worked for many years with long-term psychiatric patients in a place with a dark, sinister name derived from the Holy Inquisition. After years working with chronic patients on the ward (who, as she describes them, match chronic and sometimes explosive aspects of herself), she makes a quantum leap which enables her to resign and look for a new job with better prospects. She has a dream the night before she leaves work: she is on a lovely sunny, sandy beach in California, where there are some very large cages. I say, "It seems like an open-air zoo. A long way from where you were working before" (by which I mean the move from a closed, chronic structure, to an open one).

In the next session she tells me about one of her own patients who alternates between crises of depression and rage (he is a stalker; he winds himself up cruelly thinking about his wife's supposed unfaithfulness, and then explodes); in the same session she talks about her sister's uncontainable outbreaks of jealousy ...

After this long account, and without any explicit connection, I say, "It looks as if we've found the first inhabitants of the open-air zoo"; the furious/depressed gorilla and Othello (meaning that aspects of herself can be brought to light, described, and then put into the cages while they wait to be transformed; the game goes on for a while until a lot of cages are filled).

After some months she tells me about a visit to Paris zoo which no longer has cages but islands instead, separated by trenches, with the various animals roaming free in the islands...

But Freud didn't say this – so we can't do it.

Another aspect which keeps coming up is the necessity to find an imprimatur in Freud, who according to this research in reverse should have said or anticipated everything. If it is not possible to find such a line of descent for a concept, then that concept is not psychoanalysis.

Ideas like self-disclosure, enactment, unsaturated interpretations, and the use of characters to represent all these would not be psychoanalysis: which makes us all the more ridiculous in the opinion of those who are concerned with science, where the conceptual "caesura" is very frequent.

Another thing which seems ridiculous to me, is that in some parts of the world, psychoanalytic work is inconceivable if it does not start with a celebration of Freud and by referring to this or that point in his writings. More than anything else, this is harmful to Freud himself, who would end up being celebrated for sterility if nothing new came from his ideas. These litanies remind me of those interminable chants performed in certain religions as a homage to the divinity or a sign of belonging to the group. I can't help thinking of the way certain noble genealogies are used in some cultures: whereas in other parts of the world Freud can be quoted or not quoted without making the work better or worse, and above all, quotation has a purpose and does not represent a ritualised ora pro nobis.

Notes

1 Translator's note: This is an unconscious play on an ambiguous Italian pronoun. The patient says "*lei*" which means "her", but is also the formal "you" with which he addresses his analyst.
2 A theme underlying all these reflections is the incurable disease of "making sense", of "finding a meaning", even for things that often do not have one. And if this activity is from one point of view a peculiar and vital characteristic of our species, from another it is also its disease, because it is one thing to look for meaning and another to need to find it,

or need to have found it: which, both in the consulting room and outside it, has created dramatic situations such as those which every form of fanaticism will eventually incite. The function that operates these transformations – from the indistinct and senseless to the possibility of weaving stories, and above all of introjecting the method – is the alpha function, which besides being based on attention, receptivity, and a capacity for rêverie/re-dreaming, acquires this function of casting the mind's scenario.

4

WHAT'S HARD TO TALK ABOUT AND OFTEN GETS SAID IN WHISPERS

And the poor wretch replied!

A subject that is rarely talked about is the not uncommon breaking of the setting by the analyst with actions of a sexual nature: although it is true that Gabbard, together with Lester (1995), has often written on the topic.

It is a problem which I initially regarded as marginal, of little significance and not extensive. Over the years, with knowledge of what is happening around the world, I have realised that this is absolutely not a rare or isolated phenomenon attributable to unethical behaviour by this or that individual analyst. This is because I have seen colleagues who had been judged entirely above suspicion, of great and long experience and of manifest, proven morality, being implicated.

So, what is happening? I think we can look to a synchronic "constellation" of events – as in the death constellation (Williams, 1983) – which if present, lead to sexual action.

One undoubtedly important point is the diminution of the analyst's immune defences, which often happens at certain stages of life (masked or unacknowledged depression, or unhealthy time management by the analyst in spending long periods in contact with patients without giving enough oxygen to life outside the consulting room).

I would also add this question: are analysts satisfied and contented enough in their "real" and "sexual" lives?

It could be objected that the same question might be put to any other professional group – orthopaedic surgeons, plumbers, taxi drivers – but they do not undergo the stress of prolonged immersion in the world of fantasy, and the responsibility for bearing the burden of the mental and emotional life of someone who has entrusted these to their care.

If we are looking for a possible comparison, analysts find themselves in the same situation as radiologists whose instruments are supposed to indicate when there is an excess of radiation.

Without in any way diminishing the weight of the "individual" analyst's ethical responsibility for what happens (however the patient behaves, given that patients have the right to play their own cards in any way they like), we are led to try and consider whether, from a certain point of view, it is not possible to regard this risk as, in some way, a "professional illness".

The analyst frequently dresses in grey, wears a suit and tie, is hyper-responsible, works an incredible number of hours a day (sometimes on Fridays, Saturdays and even, in some cases, Sundays), maybe because this can act as an antidepressant. The analyst is often a workaholic.

Sometimes the gratifications he derives from all this aren't enough and, without being aware of it, he becomes first of all a healthy bearer of a sexually transmitted pathogen which sometimes explodes, as soon as other favourable factors coincide, with *incurable fever-actions* which allow no possible containment.

Can this be researched? But how? Who would available to give evidence about the early symptoms, the onset, and the acute phase of the illness and then the "tragic consequences" of almost all cases?

It is true that some Societies, the American for example, have Committees to which analysts can apply if they run into difficulties, but in these cases we are still in the preventative phase where someone has been able to recognise the warning signs – in time.

But what about "afterwards", when this has not been possible and the illness has "exploded"? What is to be done, beyond condemnation, expulsion from the IPA, and – where there is such provision from the legislative authorities – the eventual compensation of the "victim"?

I say "victim" because even patients who carry and "transmit" sexo-coccus must always and in every situation be guaranteed protection.

But how can this happen to an analyst who knows the following for certain?

- that the erotic transference is a form of negative transference;
- that the love is not intended for him, but is situational, due to what is ignited in a relationship as intimate and profound as the analytic one, while nevertheless always remaining experimental, "as if";
- that he is performing an act comparable to any other abuse, from incest to paedophilia;
- that his firefighter's training should have guaranteed that he won't be burnt, or at least that he should know how to deal with the fire, and when to put on his fireproof clothing.

Even an analyst of the front rank, author of a famous book on technique, became embroiled with Marilyn Monroe: not in terms of sexual acts, given his age, but with frequent and sensational damage to the setting.

An experienced male colleague once said to me, "It wouldn't be that bad to marry a patient. That's what they all want!" But why, I wonder, should we always speak about male analysts and female patients? Is that how it really is, or is there a still more secret kind of sexual involvement between a female analyst and a male patient?

So, when the cinema goes up in flames, as happens in a Woody Allen film, why not head for the exit? Why not take the wise decision to tell the patient that it is impossible to continue the analysis, or that it should be suspended, that there should be no contact for a while, and they should go back into the normal world of human beings?

I have no experience of these situations and have never had Circe-patients who have made me fearful, even in fantasy, about some possible action of mine. On those rare occasions when the thermometer in the field has shown a rise in temperature, I have simply interpreted it as I do any other event or communication, and both the patient and I emerge unscathed. Over time I have had recourse to metaphors that came into being on the spur of the moment.

That of the dentist: that I would be suspicious of a patient who made a sexual proposition to her dentist, but that would make me strongly suspect that she wants to avoid the pain of the drill (which implies the question: but isn't the avoidance of a badly managed and sometimes intolerable pain at the origin of many negative transferences?)

The possibility of acknowledging that the patient may turn out to be attractive, but that it is an incontrovertible "fact": if it develops within an analytic session, the fact is relevant to the analysis. If the two individuals knew each other outside, that would be another story!

If the patient had known me "outside", she is highly unlikely to have had any interest in me.

In other words, the environmental factor which enables the development of legionella-sex is the hot, moist nature of the environment in which the "treatment" (because treatment is what we are talking about) is taking place.

What analysts have not talked enough about has nevertheless been addressed by writers and film-makers.

I would like to investigate two cases: the analyst with no vocation who ends up following in the footsteps of Manzoni's Nun of Monza, and the analyst stung by that type of mosquito which now inhabits Egypt and Russia and is capable of transmitting lethal meningitis.

But how do we think about this fact in terms of the field?

Ever larger areas of the field catch fire, leading to the collapse of the field itself and the concretisation of the virtual, the only space in which analysis has meaning.

Perhaps there is a certain lack of generosity towards those who are tainted by these sins, who usually go down in the history of their group or of the psychoanalytic world as a whole because of this "fact", while everything else they have done in a long and respected professional life gets wiped out.

Maybe after a period of suspension and a ban (or if we prefer, quarantine), and if suitably treated, cured and monitored, these "unfortunates", could be readmitted to their psychoanalytic Societies, perhaps under the oversight of an ethics committee. But what I must emphasise is that we are also talking about a group illness, not one affecting only individuals, and maybe we should concern ourselves more with the question from the start, in the seminars held with trainees.

I would also be inclined to wonder if a "nun" analyst who carries a *normopathy* (the kind who are often the chosen candidates in many of the world's psycho-analytic institutes) might not run a greater risk than one who is able to maintain good relations with his own "demon".

What do trainee analysts say when they do feel able to speak?

In these notes I am not referring to the Italian Psychoanalytic Society, but to many societies in which I have had intense and long-lasting exchanges with trainees.

Trainees often complain of being led into a Zelig syndrome, where the ideal is for them to smooth themselves off to fit the other's opinion, thereby adopting a style that is offered to him as unique, instead of being helped to find, create, develop his own way of being. And this happens instead of providing a trainee with "the secret of the Rosetta stone" which would show, from both a theoretical and a technical point of view, how the various available models function.

An antidote to this disease of the "compliant trainee" would be a reading, or better still a lecture with discussion, of Bion's *Tavistock Seminars* (2005).

The trainees' revenge is often to "denounce" the trainer, as in a dictatorial regime.

Few analysts have not said or thought in their heart of hearts, "But this isn't psychoanalysis", referring to a colleague's way of thinking/working.

This can only happen to someone who has never passed beyond the boundaries of their own neighbourhood, province, region, or nation, because those who have had the good fortune to cross cultural barriers have derived great benefit from it; and if at the start they find a colleague's or a group's way of working incompre-hensible – let's say the French, or a group of colleagues in Chicago, or of neo-Freudians in New York, or very British Kleinians – at a certain point they feel that the richness of analysis is exactly this: the existence of various languages, none truer than the rest, all of them capable of meeting each other and engaging in dialogue. The languages, yes; the people less so.

Many people are sincerely convinced that there is only one right way and that the other ways are mistaken. This is like someone who works in agriculture seeing new techniques or theories and telling anyone who works in a different way, "This isn't agriculture", even going so far as to say "This isn't an olive tree or a vine!"

But all this often functions like a mirror image through which everyone thinks about other people. It is not easy to overstate how much we need to enrich our-selves with other people's points of view, but it is not enough to read them; we also need to work together, present and discuss our own and other people's sessions – and this is also very enjoyable.

Others adopt entrenched positions and when they are listening to English or Turkish, say, "But this isn't Italian, so it isn't a language!" The same thing often happens in education: in the various training institutions, the route to qualification is laid down (and until recently this was the sanctified axis of transference-coun-tertransference), whereas what we now come across is the existence of hidden lines of opposition: however, there is an antidote created by trainees, which is to give up all originality and, for any progression into a society, present work of the greatest possible neutrality and the least possible content, a strategy of "whatever you want from me" aimed at keeping as many examiners happy as possible.

How far we are from Bion, who said that there can be no Bionians because every analyst can only be himself, and suggested brief supervisions so as not to interfere with the originality and creativity of the future analyst. Now, in many of world's institutes, we are rearing battery hens, though of course there are exceptions.

Freud promised a plague when he visited the United States, and now the Chinese authorities seem happy to see psychoanalysis developing in their country because they believe it to be capable of sedating societal conflicts and dissatisfactions: from Sulphur to Opium and Incense, as befits any good religion.

Get thee behind me, Satan!

Then there are some practices that have now become official, especially in North American psychoanalysis, but which are demonized elsewhere, or at least not taken into consideration at all (outside the cultural context which produced them), condemned as non-analytic practices with no scientific debate about them: among these, I would like to record self-disclosure, the understanding of enactment, confrontation, and talking as dreaming.

Talking as dreaming

Lorena is a very "respectable" young woman, from an observant Catholic family; I am struck by the way she lies on the couch, rigid, as if turned to marble, making me think of Ilaria del Carretto sculpted above her own tomb,

One day, she is unable to take off her anorak; the zip is stuck, maybe caught in her scarf, which has itself got tangled up with her necklace, and several minutes pass before she manages to take all these things off. I feel like making an interpretation about her difficulty in revealing herself, becoming naked, showing her feelings, but I decide to keep quiet because I feel that, in these circumstances, silence is the yeast that will be able to direct the sessions towards unforeseen shores.

After some minutes of silence she says, "I saw on the internet that you have been to Istanbul. How do the women dress there?"

Here again I decide not to make one of those standard interpretations and tell her, "There's all kinds: a range from women dressed entirely in Western style with miniskirts, to those in chador, up to those in the burqa."

Lorena goes on, "What a terrible thing the burqa is for a woman, it really makes her a man's property."

I reply, "Someone told me he'd been surprised to see Arab women wearing burqas in lingerie shops."

"How strange," Lorena goes on, "I thought that under the burqa there could be a whole unknown world made of sensuality. In fact, they say that the more modest and chaste a woman seems, the more secret fantasies she has."

I say, "I was thinking about the sculpture of Ilaria del Carretto, marble, immobile. What could be underneath it?" "It's obvious," she says, "a belly dancer! And don't say anything else. That's enough for today!"

The vertex of dream-listening: film and session as dream

This concept was specifically taken up by Bion, recently recalled by Steiner, and occupies fully two chapters in the second volume of Grotstein's last book (2009), but has not been given much consideration. Or if it is attended to with interest, it is dismissed as the product of a given analyst's ability to listen at this level, and not as a practice that can be shared and transmitted (one that is probably very useful and needs to be discussed). It is usually exorcized with words like "but this doesn't take reality into account" or "this way you aren't taking real trauma into consideration".

Pilar and Lorella's husbands

The film *Take My Eyes* by Iciar Bollain is a very good description of how someone functions when they use violence in a relationship for reasons which cannot be opposed and can barely be acknowledged, a sort of incontinence and emotional dyslexia at the same time.

Watching the film may be set or regarded as an exercise. It tells the story of Pilar and her husband who, though he loves her, does so in constant fear of her being unfaithful and leaving him, so he becomes her jailer and controller.

He has a fundamentally "paranoid-abandonment" nucleus which usually stays quiet, but sometimes carries out a coup d'état and takes over, brutalising Pilar in a way he would find unthinkable when not under the influence of this "virus".

In the film he takes part in group therapy with other men who have the same problem. He is advised by one of them to keep a diary, to learn to spot the warning signals of the "emotional coup d'état", and to leave the house as soon as the crisis breaks.

Pilar's husband says that this is what happens inside him when Pilar stops being the way he wants her, when she does something unexpected that activates anxieties of abandonment and paranoiac constructions explode into violence.

And this happens to Lorella when she comes to consult me. She is happily married to Nando, except that with increasing frequency he is subject to entirely unjustified explosions of rage in which he assails her with groundless (and even ridiculous) accusations and almost reaches the point of beating her violently.

When the crisis is over he is mortified. If Lorella changes a plan or behaves differently from the way he expects, he explodes, first in the grip of suspicions, then of certainties, and so he "acts".

Lorella is really terrified by this behaviour, but here we come to a crossroads between listening as a judge, let's say, and as an analyst. The latter can only wonder where "Lorella's husband" is and when he will arrive in the session. There is no doubt that he is also (only?), from the analytic point of view, a potential functioning of the field.

Lorella begins analysis like a "lamb", always polite, scared, and gentle to the point of compliance, and we go on like this for a long time. It is an absence of mine, unexpected and unplanned, which makes the wolf, Lorella's husband, appear (at last, I would say), so that I see him explode in the session with blind rage, deaf to all evidence, seized by a sort of delusion of abandonment/jealousy/fury. Indeed, I would say that the fury is something which prevents the fragmentation of Lorella-Nando in whom suspicions of betrayal and deliberate abandonment are exploding.

The night before the next session following my return from this unavoidable break (lasting a week), I dream that a wolf (a wolf or a wolfhound?) comes into my house. Then I see that it is settling down in the sitting room while two wolf cubs and two other wolves are coming into the house. I am alarmed but not frightened, and think I should call the carabinieri and the fire service to clear my house.

Work with Lorella goes on with the growing acceptance on her part of not being only the gentle lamb but also the fierce wolf. And on her own initiative, like Pilar's husband, she starts to keep a diary which to some degree gives her a way of restraining her own emotional states with this prosthesis.

The Cabinet of Doctor Caligari

This is a silent film by Robert Wiene made in 1920. It is very interesting for a whole set of reasons.

The story is briefly that of Doctor Caligari who goes to a fair in a small town to show, among the many wonders, his "Cesare", who is 23 years old and has been asleep for 23 years. The spectacle will be that of being present at his awakening and the fact that he will be able to answer any question.

Once woken, Cesare seems to be the perpetrator of a series of savage murders, and appears to be what we would today call a serial killer.

This mode of functioning seems to respond to the commands *off*, shut down, asleep or lethargic, and *on*, uncontainably awake, a sort of Hannibal Lecter *ante litteram*.

Running briskly through the plot, we later find Doctor Caligari as the director of an asylum devoted to the study of "somnambulism" (incorrectly defined) which repeats the deeds of a certain Doctor Caligari who lived several centuries earlier, and was also interested in this subject, and who had travelled around with "his own Cesare" who had committed horrible bloodthirsty crimes. So, the madness is also, or above all, that of the asylum's director. The insanity is shared.

But the film's director has a socio-political reading of the film which stops him accepting these characteristics of his film, with which he instead aims to accuse the ruling class of insanity; so he imposes on himself the necessity of adding a small part at the beginning and another small part at the end which distort the general meaning. In fact, if we left out the introduction and finale, the whole film would be a collective delusion/dream by all the patients in the asylum, and the asylum's director would be a splendid person.

But the socio-political reading does not concern us; the madness cannot be shared, we are sane: the directors of asylums, psychiatrists, and "normal" people benefit from a sort of "judicial exemption" which protects them from any possible imputation that they too have a share in the madness. The psychoanalytic reading, however, leads us in quite another direction.

Naughtiness and destructiveness

When as adults we cannot understand a child's behaviour, especially when we have in mind a certain way for a respectable child to behave, we call this behaviour "naughty". Or else, the naughtiness is a ball of wool where we can't find the end, a ball that seems to be irritatingly tangled. So we label the tangle as "naughtiness" because we cannot weave it into any kind of sense. "Perhaps Mario will behave when ..." or "Valentina is being like this because she's cross that she and her cousin can't spend the night with their grandparents", and so on.

"Naughtiness" is a behaviour we can't get to the bottom of, often because of our lack of "intelligence". So, we use our power as adults, accusing it of being nonsense instead of making an effort (with good or bad results) to understand.

We use our power to cut off a communication which causes us anxiety because of its (apparent) obscurity. Maybe we also do this with patients, branding them with a "negative therapeutic reaction" or some other diagnosis when we aren't able to disentangle the meaning of what they are doing or saying.

Dream of the thugs

Marina is not conscious of her own rage, which she expresses in self-harm.

After a spell of analytic work, she has a dream in which "some thugs come out of her private parts". The analyst's immediate rêverie takes two forms: on the one hand, the little snakes coming out of Medusa's head and on the other, little dogs.[1] Both reveries are able to shift "rage" into a less repellent image of the thugs as "worms". But, in my opinion, this confirms that the interpretation of a dream may be a constructive transformative act.

Biol washes ...

Carlo wants an analysis because he is suffering from panic attacks and claustrophobia: he cannot travel by air or train, and cannot even use a lift because he is terrified by the idea of having no way to escape.

Gradually, violent and explosive emotions, such as jealousy, rage, vindictiveness, come into view, initially attributed to a cousin from the south, but which become ever more part of the story in each session. This "double" is sometimes deconstructed into the various explosive emotions of which he is composed. Carlo is also reticent about speaking of sexual matters, using the expression "to have Biblical relations", and is exceptionally formal in manner.

It seems clear that the symptoms are the expression of these emotions that are feared as if they were dynamite, and panic and escape routes are a way of keeping himself safe from these terrifying explosions. At this point – when he is already much better from the symptomatological point of view – he has this dream: he was in the laboratory of a shop selling dog-food, and he had to wash some dogs. But instead of dogs, there were lots of small wild animals which jumped up from everywhere, even scratching him. And there was a big zebra to wash and groom, a zebra with a big backside, and also a sheepdog with very matted fur.

Here, the deconstruction of the "double" is expressed through the description of all the wild emotions that scratch him. Here are the emotional cruxes, which he needs to untangle in the sheepdog's fur. But will he be a shepherd who can say to his analyst, "Hey, fat-arse, I could give you a good seeing to", or a shepherd who has to read the Bible yet again and keep well away from any emotional engagement?

An old advertisement used to say "Biol washes overnight": to "the dream works overnight", we could add "Night dreams and day dreams work by night and day", and the work of alphabetization goes on thanks to alpha function and night dreams.

Should I let myself go or not?

A woman patient tells me she has slept badly because of a recurring dream the previous night: she needed to go to the toilet urgently, but couldn't do a shit despite her efforts. I ask her if the dream brought anything to mind and she replies that it must have be to do with something she would like to say but can't bring herself to.

What she says exactly matches what I had been thinking, and so I tell her that maybe neither of us knows what she is holding back, but we should be able to find it together. So, we go back to a misunderstanding in the previous session and manage to clear it up, after which communication goes back to its normal fluency.

I refer to this excerpt to underline how analysis relates to communication in the *hic et nunc*, between patient and analyst and within the patient himself. It is this "communicative transgression" (I won't shit = I won't expose myself to telling you what I'm thinking; instead I'll hold back) which develops those tools for thinking that are the true goal of analysis.

Naturally, there are also other methods which end up having a therapeutic action, but which are the quickest and most effective?

In *Analysis Terminable and Interminable*, Freud (1937) writes: "Thus the real achievement of analytic therapy would be the subsequent correction of the original process of repression, a correction which puts an end to the dominance of the quantitative factor [= the force of the drives]" (p. 227).

Looking for a moment at another model, Hanna Segal (2007) states that the main therapeutic factor is "getting to know one's own unconscious" – which comes about through insight, the recovery of a good object by means of the analyst, and the correct use of the setting. Insight leads to recovery and to the reintegration of lost parts of the Ego, and knowledge replaces omnipotence.

A patient tells his analyst about a traumatic episode of constipation suffered at the age of four. The analyst probes further and postulates the nexus as being the birth of his younger brother, underlining the anal characteristics in the patient's behaviour (he does not perform – in terms of another model – the more immediately straightforward operation of understanding what the patient is holding back to an extreme extent, and why).

Another patient talks about having seen a hospital patient with scabies, little animals which bore tunnels, and then tells of having found a book about adolescence, Calvino's *The Path to the Nest of Spiders*, where there were spiders and gorges. Invited to say more about this, she says, "I can't connect things, I've got no imagination," and adds, "there aren't any important things to say today."

But developing the *dreaming ensemble* (Grotstein, 2007) means developing these abilities, and so I tell her that the very fact that there aren't any important facts allows us to inquire into those annoying and far from clear thoughts that are under the skin or in the gorges, to be looked at with irritation and a certain repulsion. "I wouldn't know what to say," she replies, although she adds a rapid sequence of half-hidden "annoying" thoughts which thus gain citizens' rights and identity cards (they are identifiable and acquire the right to be acknowledged and to have somewhere to live).

But, in my opinion, what matters is the development of the dreaming ensemble, and certainly not of the contents, from which the veil of repression can be removed.

But here we meet the problem of "the analysts' compulsion to repeat", because analysts often act – if not exactly like Molière's doctors with enemas and blood-letting – then like old surgeons who can't resign themselves to the use of endoscopy.

Fear and psychoanalysis

A feeling – or rather an emotion or an affective state, which can be inhaled in many psychoanalytic institutions in Italy and abroad – is fear, and it takes many forms.

It could represent, for example, the *denial of time*. It has many precipitates which stem from thinking we are "young trainees at the age of 45" or "young trainers at 65", but this is not the most disquieting aspect, which is that we put psychoanalytic theories into a still, or rather, circular time in which everything has been said, so that nobody can say or ever could have said it better. This blocks any new approach and makes it heterodox, even blasphemous. The scientists of psychoanalysis who had to carry the plague of new knowledge have been transformed into clerics and officiating priests of known, very well known, theories now lacking any therapeutic efficacy for many of the pathologies we have to address today.

But the diagnosis had been made before by Bion: it is terror of the new, the unknown, that leads to the exaltation of the known. We are afraid of what we do not know about the mind (and about our own minds) and this makes us take refuge in the self-congratulatory *kyrie eleisons* of much psychoanalysis: the phases (oral, anal, phallic), the primal scene, castration anxiety, penis envy and so on, which are no longer of any use – if they ever were – except as "stoppers" to try and cover the black holes of our not-knowing.

What do two minds produce together? Where do they go? What do they – and what could they – create? Everything that does not fit into the ritualised known is condemned and branded with the familiar anathema "But this isn't psycho-analysis!" – regardless of whatever (almost) everyone else will say.

But fear can even lead to denial of the evidence: of the fact that there are dif-ferent "models" of psychoanalysis. Instead, a single psychoanalysis is supposed to exist with various modes of expression or interpretation; this arises out of ignorance and failure to participate in or associate with working groups unlike one's own, and is likewise the product of fear of what we do not know. In Italy we often hear people say, "But American psychoanalysis isn't psychoanalysis", without ever having worked with American colleagues.

Fear stops psychoanalysis budding as it should and as it has the potential to do. In a lecture given in Milan, Paolo Fonda said:

> Freud, our common forefather, is a pretty strong model for identification, a high-energy device that needs careful handling. In any family, a brilliant father is a big problem for the children. An excessive idealisation of him can create a burdensome internal object that is not easy to live with. And if we also consider him our main theoretical and clinical point of reference, we risk undervaluing everyone who has come after him, contributing to the growth and richness of psychoanalysis. [And let's not forget that over 90% of analysts in the IPA have worked, researched, theorised and published after 1939.] The group is in danger of establishing a foundation myth of a father unable to produce children capable of equalling him, of becoming real, productive adults in their own turn. That could then support a vertical group function in which the old are forever superior to the eternally immature young, and can never be matched by them. [...] This echoes the set-ups in the Catholic Church, and in feudal and communist systems: three heavy-weight producers of mass infantilization. Infantilization and anti-democracy in fact turn out to be synonymous.
>
> *(2012, n.p.)*

This fear which leads to the denial of time, of development, or of "catastrophic changes", and is due to various shifts of model, (in my case, I would say Freud ⇢ Klein ⇢ Bion ⇢ ?), also leads to a denial of space (that is, of other places where other models hold sway) and then becomes fear inside the training institutions where everything gets mothballed: including the "candidates" or "pupils", call them what you will. The admissions process in all societies is often more like a Holy Inquisition than a test of the examinee's ability, creativity and independence.

Originality is a word we don't hear uttered, even when scientific works are being chosen for publication, and those that are tend instead to be a litany of the known and very well-known. Whatever is original smells instantly of heterodoxy and must be sterilised.

An idea of "immutability" seems opposed to that natural transience of scientific models which constantly reminds us of our own transience: whereas many psychoanalytic institutions have created *Kinderheime* for the middle-aged, who are happy to live in them, performing now meaningless rituals.

The white coat and neutrality

For some years now, doctors in psychiatric services and hospital departments have been tending more and more to wear the white coat.

This had almost disappeared in the seventies, a sign that the "barrier" between psychiatric patient and clinician had fallen. The new custom, rich in implicit communications, lasted for years until almost all doctors, for the best of motives, gradually re-appropriated the white coat with its connotations of a sharp caesura, separation, differentiation, freedom from contamination, professional status, the opposition between ill and healthy, and so on. There are a thousand cogent and practical reasons for doing this (hygiene, recognisability, professional status, etc.) but that is another subject.

I want to address a different question: is there an equivalent of the white coat in the analytic consulting room?

I think there is: to start with, the uniform worn by many analysts, the often compulsory and highly formal suits – mostly a sober jacket and tie for men and outfits low on colour for women (for an example, see the analyst in Polanski's ad for Prada, easily available on YouTube).

But there is a still more powerful uniform, the analyst's so-called "neutrality" which, while it is for the most part now considered inadmissible and obsolete, in fact remains on the scene through the analyst's introjection of inveterate habits and modes of behaviour: not responding to the patient's legitimate questions or needs but, even more, being terrified of letting oneself be "contaminated" by the patient's emotions and hence viewing with horror those practices – of which one has no knowledge or experience – established in many psychoanalytic models which go beyond a benign acceptance of "co-thinking" or co-construction, and which really put the analyst's mental, emotional and affective life into play, such as certain technical modalities of American psychoanalysis – from the extreme endorsement of enactment (while in Europe its substantial difference from acting-out and acting-in is undervalued) to indiscriminate self-disclosure, though used in a specific technical application, or provoking direct confrontation.

These practices are greatly abhorred because they remove one's "neutrality", our "psychic white coat" cut from the privileged cloth of Freudian metapsychology studied and learned from aseptic paper texts, which shields and protects us from the evacuations, haemorrhages, and living, polluting emotions of the "patient", rather than "our secret travelling companion".

Note

1 Translator's note: Miranda's word is "*cagnotti*" which mostly indicates "tough guys" in service as bodyguards, enforcers, etc. It is also a diminutive of *cani*, dogs.

5

EVACUATIVE AND PSYCHOSOMATIC PATHOLOGIES

In the light of a post-Bionian model of the mind

Introduction

In evacuative manifestations (hallucinations, behaviours involving no substantial thought, and psychosomatic symptoms) elements of sensoriality (which have been neither contained nor transformed) can be evacuated into the body. We could think of this symptom as the dehydrated precipitate of a dream it has not been possible to dream (Ogden, 2009; Ferro, 2009).

The problem will be: what type of dream will it be possible to have about these elements, whose evacuation has after all enabled the best possible mental functioning in the circumstances? So, we have to reckon with the fact that on the one hand evacuation is a successful defence mechanism, while on the other it leads to a symptom. In this chapter, I shall devote most of my attention to psychosomatic manifestations.

"Bridge-building" between mind and body is certainly problematic. I tend to think it best to keep a firm hold on our capacity for narrative and consider how often an immersion in the analytic "dream-pool" produces effects. Sometimes, on the other hand, everything seems to make sense but the reality of the body stays unchanged. At other times, if it is eased by the infiltrations of the proto-mental, bodily reality starts to function again. From this perspective we have to admit that there is a whole transformative process which runs from proto-sensoriality to symbolisation, from evacuation to dream.

In Bionian jargon I would say that alongside the evacuation of beta elements, we have the evacuation of balpha and alpha elements.

In this way we move from evacuations that lead to psychosomatic pathologies, to evacuations that have scraps of meaning, to evacuations clearly endowed with sense. It is as if, working backwards, what had been projected were:

a   segments of film;
b   a few partly ruined stills;
c   the celluloid the film is made from.

Naturally, there are ascending degrees of difficulty, and it is not the case that once the psyche-soma wall has been breached, it can be rebuilt by work "further upstream" (the wall approximates to what, in the jargon, we call the contact barrier), even though sometimes we can't help thinking it can.

Andrea, an eight-year-old boy brought for a consultation, bursts into floods of tears whenever he finds himself in a situation where he fears he won't know what to do.

In a way, it is a form of "enuresis" through the eyes, or rather a form of incontinence which leads to a lessening of tensions by means of evacuation. Analytic work with him will lead to the reconstituting of his capacity for containment.

As Andrea becomes interested in the various types of relationship between "mothers and new-born babies" in other species, and in the details of the bond between them, lions and tigers start to appear, the sessions take place in the forest, and then Viking warriors arrive.

Complex emotions will be alphabetised and contained without the continuing presence of the symptom.

We are aware that we are only tangentially concerned with the symptom but with the dysfunction of what lies upstream from it.

When what is upstream gets restructured, sometimes what lies downstream disappears. Some of the highly significant symptoms are:

• enuresis (where the theme is uncontainability);
• mutism (where most of the time the theme is the muzzle placed on Hannibal Lecter or on Munch's screamer: that is, hyper-continence);
• dyslexia, where the problem is the subverting of the basic emotional grammar, which leads to a failure to recognise concave / ($♀$) and convex / ($♂$): in other words, the first and necessary discrimination between different emotional letters/readings.

How far can we venture on this journey? I would say, in fantasy a long way; with reason as far as no man's land, the unknown and little loved land of "we don't know"!

At this point it is inevitable that I should briefly refer to my model, which arises from the meeting of the post-Bion model with the Barangers' post-field model.

Bion

With Bion (1962; 1963; 1965; 1997) we have a revolution comparable to the French Revolution: after it, nothing is as it was before. The pivotal point is therefore that the unconscious is in a perpetual state of formation/transformation and that it is secondary and subsequent to the relationship with the Other.

Nameless dreads, proto-sensorialities, and projected proto-emotions evacuated into the Other's mind are transformed into alpha elements by the digestive-metabolic function of this other (caregiver – alpha functions as a whole – analyst): in other words, of the field. These are illustrated tiles (pictograms) (but they can also draw on all the other senses) which when linked together bring waking dream-thought to life. Alpha elements are then continually repressed, establish the ability to remember – and hence to forget – and form the "contact barrier" which is the limit that interposes between conscious and unconscious. This is well known. What is less often considered, though Neri (2006), Ogden (2007) and Grotstein (2007) hint at it, is the fact that some beta elements infiltrate the picture and escape the process of alphabetisation. In my opinion, these are the centre of interest in analysis: that is, those *quanta* of proto-emotion and of sensoriality which have never been transformed.

These are the quanta which constitute those tsunamis, cyclones, and sou'westers of beta elements which – if not sufficiently transformed – give rise to the most severe pathologies.

At the origin of the image

In psychoanalysis the realm of the image is the dream. Perhaps we should say "has been", at least since Bion provided us with a model of the mind in which there is a constant forming of images (which, with Rocha Barros, 2000, we could call pictograms) by a function called alpha which continually operates to transform into images all the sensoriality which pervades it, no matter where it comes from.

Where some of these pictograms are projected into the outside world, they would maintain their characteristic oneiric quality and would constitute the visual flashes which Meltzer often spoke about, as I have after him (Ferro, 1992).

Another example in which projection occurs with greater violence and where we are in the field of *transformations in hallucinosis*, would be that of a patient who projects pictograms onto someone in order to adopt them afterwards as characteristics entirely belonging to the other.

But let's go back to explaining the model of the mind I am referring to: during the day we will have built up an enormous stockpile of pictograms (alpha elements) and so it would be the job of a "super alpha function" to effect a sort of second pressing/weaving of these stockpiles, so as to create the dream images which would be the most digested product of our thinking apparatus.

The great difference between "conversion" and "somatisation" in my model is that while in the former we have the discharge of balpha elements and hence their correlatives in the form of fragments of derived narratives, in the latter we have the evacuation of "pure" beta elements which have not initiated processes of mentalisation and metabolisation (Grotstein, 2007).

While the former bring with them some *quanta* of "thinkability" or proto-pictograms and proto-sequences of balpha, along with possible immature chains of derived narratives, the latter have undergone no process of mentalisation (Ferro, 2002b; 2005a; 2009).

Moreover, while the analyst can find that he is able to give scraps of meaning to the former, with the latter he is confronted by the problem which lies upstream: i. e. the fact that there is a marked, although inconsistent, defectiveness, in the tools which lead to mentalisation.

When pure beta elements are evacuated, it is as if we were in a theatre with neither light nor sound, in the presence of a broken pipe constantly evacuating sewage; where these coalesce, they give rise to various psychosomatic pathologies.

If the evacuation happens at a later stage, we have a penumbra and minimal sonic interference, which allows us to try and construct a meaning: in other words, it is actually possible to work on the contents (whereas in the first case the work must be done upstream of the contents). Naturally, there can be pathologies affecting points further along the way to mentalisation.

Projective identification is that natural attempt to relieve the mind by projecting disturbing states caused by fragments of sensoriality into the mind of the Other. If the other is receptive, he will not only be permeable to these fragments, not just giving the sense of dimensionality (depth), but also the sense of temporality due to the relatively foreseeable alternation between concave and convex: added to the receptivity will be the capacity for transformation and progressive alphabetisation of the projected (beta) elements which, once transformed (alpha) will become the building blocks of thought.

Recently the biggest change in psychoanalysis has been the shift from attention to the contents of the mind to attention to the development of tools that will enable thought, feeling, dreaming.

From this perspective, the two key points involved in the development of a mind would be the development of the container and the *dreaming ensemble*: that is, of all those activities concerned with what Grotstein (2007) calls the *dreaming ensemble*, consisting of all the mind's dreaming functions: alpha function, reverie, night dreams, and super alpha function (Grotstein, 2007; 2009).

Ogden (2009) considers the symptom, any symptom, as the product of an undreamed dream: in other words, an accumulated scar tissue of beta elements which can find various defence mechanisms (hence, symptoms) to seal them off while they wait to be de-concretised, and finally dreamed. This dream would correspond to a process of digestive metabolisation which, through the formation of unconscious images (pictograms), would set in motion the first elements of thought-emotion like a two-sided coin

Reverie can take a variety of forms: a flash when it is instantaneous, a feature film when it arises out of a connection between different moments of reverie, and lastly that continual activity of receptive/ transformative work done without our being aware of it.

Closely linked to this idea are the curative, therapeutic factors which have been differently described in different models.

Analytic field

What I am talking about always takes place within that structure called a field, in which I could say that the analytic session appears like a dream of the minds to which refracted and overlapping stories come from times and places that are different from the field itself (Ferro and Basile, 2009). The shared experience is that of allowing emotional states, affects, thoughts and characters to circulate, with the analyst (who is also a place in the field) guaranteeing and safeguarding the setting, and promoting an activity of an oneiric kind on the part of the analytic pair.

The session is played out on the level of a mutual dream, both when the patient "dreams" (if he is able to) the analyst's intervention and mental state, and when the analyst "dreams" the response to be given to the patient. The more this response is "dreamed", the more it will be a factor in constituting, knitting together again, the likely deficiency in the patient's alpha function.

From one point of view, the analytic field is that "unsaturated waiting room" where emotions, proto-emotions, and characters stay until they can be brought back to their saturated destiny, in the relationship and in the construction.

From another point of view, the field is made by all the lines of force, all the proto-clusters of proto-emotions, proto-characters, and characters which float in the virtual space of the field, gradually acquiring density, colour, and three-dimensionality.

As if a lot of elastic bands, possible storylines, were stretching between patient and analyst, and little by little names start to hang them from them on paperclips, as casting which the field makes out of what had been undetermined.

In this latter model of the field which aims to become an oneiric field, what matters is the development of the field's dreaming abilities, which will lead to the transformation and introjection of functions.

In the field we have unconscious or unmentalised functioning, continually transformed into the thinkable through the phenomenon of casting and through transformation in dream.

In this model, the fulcrum of the analysis is the development of the ability to dream and not just the work of repression or splitting.

But if we are to penetrate a hypothesis which I find convincing, we need some additional contributions in line with the researches of Norman (2001) and Salomonsson (2007).

Basic emotional grammar

In many pathologies we have an alteration of the basic emotional grammar, which is organised according to simple sequences of concave/ convex:

UU∩ ... UU∩∩UUU ...

This basic grammar consists of the alternation between receptive and penetrative which forms the emotional basis of every more complex emotional-affective grammar: you accept me/you reject me/I accept you/I reject you.

The basis is given by the continual interplay of *projective identifications* and *reverie*. This rhythmic pattern remains as the base fabric which tends to establish itself and on which the experiences that follow the organisation of the basic rhythm are laid down like veils and, in due course, like a carpet.

A patient expresses all this through the progressive use of the *ba-th* where he will find this receptive space, and where he will be able to evacuate anxieties (Meltzer's toilet-breast).

Then the nourishing convex space of the elegant *ba-r* will appear, offering a wide range of cakes. Then the *ba-rrier* will appear, marking the limit and then modulating into a *ba-ng* during outbursts of rage.

And so we will have:

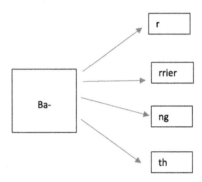

the fruit of the rhythmic journey between projection and reception.

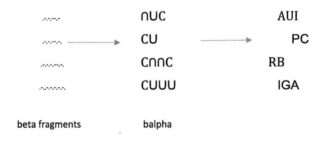

At this point, a further complexification is simple. But, for a long time, these proto-structures will signal the development of the type of mental functioning. This one will signal what type of mental functioning is taking place.

A problem can be caused by an excess of convexity:

∩∩∩∩∩∩∩∩∩ (absence of reverie/ receptiveness)

or by an excess of receptiveness:

UUUUUUUU (absence of ♂ and of turbulence)

but also by a dissociation between the content of the deep sequence, for example ∩∩∩∩∩∩∩,

and the signals which come from other channels: a mother who is mentally blocked and yet smiles, which is the basis of many pathologies, especially the "three Ds" (dyslexia, dysgraphia, dyscalculia).

One exercise could be to draw the base sequence of these affective codes.

3-Ds syndrome

I have already described what I would call "3-Ds syndrome" *caused by a failure to share emotional states*: that is, when there is a lack of that basic shared emotional grammar on which all emotional syntax is built, and likewise any possibility of reading and calculating, or of feeling an appropriate sense of belonging – an emotional sharing which activates the ability to read, predict, and calculate one's own and other people's emotions.

If this emotional "slab of reinforced concrete" is missing, cracked, uneven, etc., every layer of cognitive and interpretative carpet will suffer from the underlying pathology. Hence we will have the most diverse cognitive-behavioural symptomatology, including the possible varieties of dyslexia, dyscalculia, dysgraphia.

What I would call "3-Ds syndrome" *complicated by injections of rage and deficiency of reverie* comes about in a different way: this is that particular form in which not only is there a deficit of intuition and emotional harmony, but also a projection of rage that is not transformed because there is insufficient reverie function. Alphabetisation happened further upstream, and the damage is at earlier levels (that is, not just in the concrete slab but in the load-bearing structures beneath it).

Stefano gives us an example of this second mode.

He is a boy of 13 brought to analysis by his parents because of his difficulties in reading and writing. His parents had not noticed this until it was reported by the school.

They say, *en passant*, that he loves very violent films and has bulimic tendencies. Perhaps, the parents explain, he has been referred because of an often-unmanageable rage and fury. He is very close to a slightly younger cousin, Maura, who is affected by elective mutism. Once a psychotherapeutic treatment has been agreed, he starts to create cartoon strips (he is very talented at drawing) in which various characters gradually come to life, such as Genghis Khan, a robot, and in particular two violent and uncontainable characters called "Slash" and "Tomahawk".

It is not my intention to expatiate on Stefano's therapy, but to underline certain points.

The bond with Maura immediately suggests the bond between incontinence and hyper-continence, while the violent films, Genghis Khan, Slash and Tomahawk lead us to the projective, evacuative aspect of rage which strikes at meanings, connections, and links, severing them from each other and fragmenting them in such a way that it becomes difficult and sometimes impossible to perform operations with and on them. The "slash", "/", seems to delete certain letters; the tomahawk seems to chop up fragments of meaning; the overeating seems to add cream and cake, and to smooth over the corners (as if Rottweilers were being so overfed that they were turning into fat cattle).

Because of which, illustrating it in linguistic terms, the destiny of a phrase or letters which accompany it would derive from the graphical agglutinations which are formed: if he wrote an E, this would be covered and made unrecognisable by an R (rage) + a slash / + T for Tomahawk + O from stodge = something illegible.

We would complexify this example – which is only useful as an illustration – in relation to any letter, word, or phrase, or emotion, if we posit the initial E as standing for Emotion.

Which leads in narrative terms to an advertisement for the old television programme *Carosello* in which an animated character arriving in a modern city from a primitive world became disoriented and said, "Me not know, I am a stranger, squares, triangles, stripes on the ground", showing that he did not understand the (road) signs which were comprehensible to everyone else and helped them find their way around.

We could say that is a matter of pathologies in which one is a "stranger" to the other's mind and to one's own, and so in the absence of shared signs one gets lost. "It's all grist to the mill" the advert went on, suggesting there is no differentiation of meanings and that sense has no value.

In the first session Stefano has a dream in which there are brief excerpts from "Three men and one leg", the title of a successful comic film, but which speaks about the need to integrate the pieces, and then he starts talking about "Nintendo", which immediately seems to home in on the topic of "not understanding",[1] of indecipherable signs: triangles, squares, and lines on the ground.

I would add that the person who agrees to take Stefano in to therapy has a dream after a few sessions in which he was going to fetch Stefano from the paediatrician's waiting room and took him to a sofa where he hugged him along with his own children.

Let's now try to see what are the implications in clinical practice of this model which is interesting more and more researchers, although with one peculiarity: it is a model of the mind applicable to all ages, and can be used independently of considerations of sex, age, and specific circumstances (naturally as far as the base facts of the model are concerned; logically, there are variables alongside the invariants, such as different expressive registers – for example, in the analysis of children. See Ferro and Basile, 2009).

Dyslexia, enuresis, elective mutism

Emotional dyslexia: Renata and the vacuum cleaner

Renata asks for a consultation because, getting annoyed by her eldest child, an eight-year-old daughter, while she was doing the housework, she had hit her on the head with the vacuum cleaner. The girl was admitted to A & E, and the mother cannot get over what has happened.

She tells me more about her children: the second child, a boy, suffers from enuresis, while the youngest, also a boy, has nightmares. The eldest daughter suffers from dyslexia. So, it appears clear at the start, from a "field" perspective, that the leitmotif is that of (emotional) incontinence, a leitmotif made all the more complex by "dyslexia": in other words, the inability to read, recognise, distinguish, name, and connect proto-emotional states and emotions.

In addition, the second child suffers from asthma, and it is obvious – in the dreamed field – that asphyxiating hyper-continence is present as a possible defence mechanism. Renata goes to say that as a child she too was unable to read and that, because of this, she had tantrums in which she would fling herself onto the ground in a kind of hyper-motor crisis. The "flinging herself onto the ground" later appears in a scene with her depressed husband, who spends a lot of time in bed. She tells me it is impossible for her to put letters together.

At this point, a brief digression is called for: why would someone take this as evidence of an intolerance to the primal scene or as an envious attack on the couple? Wouldn't it be simpler to think in terms of an inability to read emotions and connect them to each other, precisely because they haven't been alphabetised and because of the "dyslexia" associated with them?

In subsequent sessions, Renata will talk about a series of miscarriages suffered by her sister and cousin, picking up the theme of incontinence. Evacuation is possible and perhaps there can be no better metaphor for the inversion of alpha function than the vacuum cleaner which, instead of "sucking in", violently strikes the other (or the other parts of herself).

In the first phase of the work, she always adds "my joy" as a kind of obligatory suffix to the names of her children. For example, Raul "my joy", which sounds like an exorcism against rage and weariness and the "swearword" she'd like to shout. After a while, however, we meet the primary school teacher who patiently taught her to read, and one day Renata says, "Now I'm learning to give a name to the things I feel", and she does indeed become able to "connect up her emotions" while describing her daughter as being able to join up letters, syllables and starting to read short sentences.

The Minotaur who turned to wood

Salvatore is brought to therapy for an elective "mutism" which started and grew steadily worse after his parents separated. His mother has left the family and gone to live with a new partner. After a short period in which Salvatore seemed to have adapted to the new situation, he started to suffer from enuresis (the theme of incontinence again) and shortly afterwards stopped speaking at school (hyper-continence).

In the first meetings he doesn't say a word. He looks worn out, and seems to rock. It occurs to the analyst to suggest that Salvatore might whisper some words to his father who accompanies Salvatore to the session and takes part in the observation, and thus begins to act as a loudspeaker. Salvatore whispers some words to his father, who repeats them, amplified and audible.

The first structured game which appears is that of the zoo, where tigers, lions, and gorillas are shut up in very strong cages.

The second game is that of a very fierce dog which has to be muzzled.

The analyst finds himself thinking about the story of Agent Starling and Hannibal Lecter, who is kept in a kind of muzzle to stop him catching and biting people.

It seems clear that behind this kind of "mutism" – or rather the "reduction of phonatory volume to the minimum" – there is incontinence of the kind very well portrayed by Munch in *The Scream*.

It is not only abandonment by his mother which leaves Salvatore without words, but also her total lack of warmth and closeness to him. The comment his mother had made thinking back to Salvatore's birth had been, "He's always been a weight on me and an obstacle to my career, which I had always dedicated my life to and wanted to go on doing so."

After some months of therapy Salvatore agrees that his father can leave the room and wait in the lobby. In order to develop his game, he agrees to write down what his "characters" need from time to time to communicate in the game, while the analyst will provide the voices for other characters. I think it is important to understand the defensive set-up of "hyper-continence" as an alternative to incontinence.

This is because it allows us to work on the deconstruction of the emotional tsunami that is feared to be devastating. We will be able to proceed with a deconstruction of this tsunami into many different winds-emotions (sou'wester, Alpine, sirocco …) corresponding to equivalent emotions that need to be deciphered (rage, jealousy, abandonment).

Or, changing the metaphor, we could say that, from this perspective, it is helpful to proceed with the development of a container and the figure of a "wild animal tamer" who could guarantee that fierce animals (emotions and proto-emotions) can roam free and yet be contained (not hyper-contained!) by this new function. This will allow them to be modulated.

Note

1 Translator's note: "Nintendo" suggests "*non intendo*" – "I don't understand".

6

WEAVING THOUGHTS AND IMAGES IN MY OWN WAY

Introduction

This is a rather a particular chapter in which I would like to give a disorganised but honest account of the analyst's day to day work, which I think is well represented by the image beneath (Figure 6.1), where we clearly see the activity of knitting together undifferentiated sensoriality, which in the drawing has already reached the level of the syllable, so that it can be written down in a narrative framework: in the end we just have to know how to knit and use the right needles for the job. But the picture could also be seen as going in the opposite direction, towards a deconstruction that is capable of bringing release from the obligation to reiterate modes of being, until we create a bundle of micro-narremes that can be woven together in completely new and unpredictable ways.

Narratives and images: Viviana's mice

There is a period of relative impasse with Viviana which authorises me to highlight the fact that, even though we have been acquainted for quite some time, I know very little about her, and that I wouldn't mind being granted a bit more admittance to her and her world every now and then.

In the next session she tells me two dreams.

In the first she arrives in a place where she sits down on a sofa, and there are armchairs, upright chairs, and a table. She is lying down comfortably when she feels something moving in the cushion she is resting on, and suddenly sees swarms of black mice running in groups.

Then the dream changes and she is in a similar place, but this time there are some people sitting around the room and at a certain point she understands that they are mummified, embalmed, as in a museum of waxworks.

It is not hard for me to refer these two dreams back to my having urged Viviana the day before to consider making me more of a participant in her world. This has caused a commotion: all the mice, the black memories, the gloomy atmospheres of her childhood have sprung up in a way she feels as menacing, troubling, but not terrifying.

Yet the alternative seems even worse: a world where everything has stopped, timeless or outside time, like in a waxworks museum or Roald Dahl's story *The Landlady*, set in a small hotel where nothing happens, nothing is transformed or evolves, and the occasional young guest will discover to his cost the horrible and immutable destiny that awaits him.

Viviana is struck by what I tell her and takes it on board, rewriting these scenes in her own words and with her own experiences, so that she can then arrive at the fact that her father – with whom there has been no contact for years – has turned up at her mother's house and asked about her; then she tells me she has met up again with a male schoolfriend with whom she would like to re-establish a relationship.

The medication (drug)-characters

Some characters in the session often function as drugs. Amelia is married to Carlo, with whom she leads a tedious, uneventful life, and so she has a lover, Goffredo, whom she meets twice a week in an outburst of intense passion. But Amelia cannot entirely give up either man: one guarantees stability, security, acts I would say as an old lifeguard, while the other electrifies her with erotic excitement. The former functions as a base to lean on, a stabiliser, the latter as an antidepressant.

What will become steadily clearer is the impossibility for Amelia of giving up either one of these drugs: she would plunge into a void or into depression.

This kind of drug has enabled her to avoid contact with the Little Match Girl who can't swim.

Over time, if all goes well, these drug-characters will become functions performed by the analyst (and before that by the field itself) in order subsequently to become the patient's mental legacy.

Drug-characters are more frequent than one might think: one of their characteristics is their interchangeability (one can stand in for another, depending on the role to be performed). Moreover, if the analysis is working, they are steadily "set loose", becoming functions carried out by the field and then introjected.

The psychosomatic malady

The psychosomatic malady and its origins can be described using many different metaphors. One might be that of a sheet of paper screwed into a ball and evacuated into the body, after which it has to be smoothed out and interpreted by reading what is written on it.

Another might be the procedure of "zipping" a document or image, which in its compressed form could block a function of the computer until it is unzipped and allowed to circulate.

In the jargon with which I am most comfortable, this is a matter of beta and balpha elements which compose aggregated masses evacuated into the soma, giving rise to illnesses which only a reversal of the process – when this is possible – will be able to cure. Put another way, we will have to construct a field high in reverie and increasingly able to suck back these unmetabolized or untransformed elements into alpha elements (pictograms), dreams, and emotional thoughts.

Our mental is not integrated into our corporeal. The mental has interfered in a fundamentally well-functioning equilibrium. The same holds true for sexuality: it is the mental which has disturbed and interfered with a sexuality that would otherwise have been healthy.

Examination dreams

During the admissions procedure for training analysis (a job I have done in many psychoanalytic Societies because of the various roles I have found myself fulfilling over the years) one candidate tells her interviewers the following dream: she was at a bus stop where the bus was about to arrive, and did not know if the driver would let her get on. She had a large daisy in her hand and started pulling off the petals.

Another candidate introduces himself to the panel by telling them he has a brain tumour with pulmonary metastases; he is in chemotherapy but certain to be cured because his cancer can only be "psychosomatic in nature". He takes morphine daily for the recently appeared metastases in his bones. In a dream he had the night before the interview, he had to go to a party, a big celebration in his honour prepared by friends and relations, but first of all he to spend three important hours talking with three analysts. Only after this would he be happy to go to the party being held in his honour.

Neither dream seems to require much commentary. They recount in real time the experience of the interview: the first full of expectations and hopes, the second a tragic epilogue with the description of the dreamer's own funeral.

In a selection interview for admission to a school of psychotherapy, a young woman appears at the appointed time and as she walks towards the chair in my studio announces in ringing tones, "I am Emilia." Just as she is sitting down I say to her, "And so tell me about Romagna!"[1]

She immediately understands the meaning of my intervention, saying, "I intuit that you are not interested in what I already know about myself, and are interested in all those things I don't really know, the things that are confused and obscure." The interview continued, but she had already gained her place at the psychotherapy school by catching my joke "in flight".

The inability to be alone

A patient has a dream after many years of analysis: a little girl has been left alone on a pavement. She is attracted by something on the opposite side of the road and is walking towards it when she is run over by cars, vans, maybe lorries. It isn't clear if she was dead or alive, and at this point the patient goes away with her own young daughter, holding her hand, as an ambulance arrives. This patient clearly has a functioning part which she is evidently able to look after (the girl whose hand she holds) and a part which, when it is abandoned (between one session and another), is run over by the emotions of rage, exclusion, shame, embarrassment. Her problem is now one of self-esteem which develops well when things go smoothly but is knocked down during every "break", such as the weekend or holidays, or the analyst's incomprehension.

By contrast, another patient who is much more seriously ill has the following dream over the weekend: "they arrive on Saturday, the bastards, they're often drunk, they knock everything over". It might seem like a delusion – it has that flavour – but why not consider it from the point of view of its content, as the same communication as that being made by the previous patient, but by a patient who as yet has inadequate tools for managing the arrival of the "bastards": that is, of those mental states that risk dismantling her – in other words, those emotions or rather proto-emotions which might "blow up her very apparatus for thinking"?

These last two topics take cinematic narrative form in *I Am Legend* by Francis Lawrence (2007) in which the last surviving human finds himself alone in a deserted New York where, in the clefts and recesses of old shops, mutant monsters are surviving, coming out at sunset to look for food. At sunset all the protagonist can do is hide in an apartment which the mutants won't find as long as they don't discover its location. In this film the loneliness and the monsters which become active at twilight are described in an unforgettable manner, as often happens in science fiction films and books when a particularly sensitive chord is touched – as has been the case from *The Invasion of the Body-Snatchers* by Don Siegel (1956) to *Alien* by Ridley Scott (1979).

Tarzan and the crocodile

Lorena works in a pharmacy, but what pharmaceuticals does she need? The story she tells is of depression in the family, her father's, her mother's and her brother's, and her sister's panic attacks and obsessionality. She lives without passion with Giovanni, but is deeply in love with Samyr, a colleague she has known since university, and with whom she secretly spends a lot of time, in a romantic and mutual idealisation but without any full sexual relations. It seems that Samyr arrived like a mild antidepressant able to mitigate her experience of depression – although the problem of depression, emotional incontinence (panic), and *claustrum* (obsessionality) seems to need more substantial interventions. It is at this point that she comes to analysis. Her first dream takes place in a dark night. She is a girl balancing precariously on the back of a crocodile which might go under the water at any moment, with the double risk of drowning Lorena (because she can't swim) or devouring her. However, there is also a figure, part swimming instructor part Tarzan, who seems to be approaching with – she hopes – the intention of helping her and the ability to do so.

Work in progress

Once a patient has developed a more secure and fruitful relationship with her analyst she dreams about being in a limousine driven by a homosexual friend as her friend Amalia is marrying an Ethiopian. There is also a little boy in the car.

Obviously, out of context this dream could be telling us a thousand different stories. But one interpretative exercise could be a graphical transcription in a hypothetical field, with all of the field in a state of expansion:

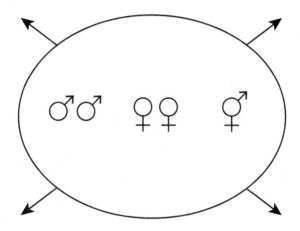

This could tell us about a marriage between – or rather, the coming together – the functioning of the patient and her analyst, or between functions of the patient which were at first distant and split.

It could tell us about something undifferentiated that is nevertheless being born (a child) and lastly about a function of the field which has not yet unfolded and been sufficiently accepted. But many stories could be developed from this: what will become of all these protagonists? It all depends on how the field's next movements pan out.

It might be a useful exercise to draw a few graphs setting out what happens in a session in terms of (provisionally) designing the field (Ferro, et al., 2013).

A song by Dalida had the title *A ma manière*: this part of the chapter develops the theme of the song's title. Without too many theories, or only implicitly, I shall take the reader into my kitchen to share my experience of being at the stove. This has the further advantage that it is also possible, using clinical material that has not been metapsychologically over-elaborated, to practise all the different ways of seeing it, which is a panacea that can relativise our supposed truths and beliefs.

The chill of death and the electric blankets

The culture of the human species (which leads us to suffer or rejoice in a professional success or because of a child's bad mark at school) is the most elaborate and cosiest blanket for warming us up when chilled by the awareness of our extreme finitude. We use other, less sophisticated "blankets" such as faiths and religions, which have the same function but have a deleterious effect on our capacity for thought, whereas the "culture-blanket" develops and enriches our set of tools for thinking.

At the same time as it protects us, the culture we belong to gives us an experience like that described in the film *The Truman Show* by Peter Weir (1998) where the protagonist lives, without knowing it for a long time, inside a bubble of virtual reality which protects and isolates him.

The same goes for cultures in general, including the faiths and sub-faiths of psychoanalysis which end up performing the same function.

At a recent IPA Congress in Mexico City (2011) which had, exceptionally, been opened to university students, one of them who was on a panel I was chairing asked if it was possible to development the alpha function by the use of electricity. Needless to say, everyone laughed to the utter humiliation of the poor speaker. I returned to this intervention during the closing panel and said that I found it brilliant. Not in the literal sense, but in the sense that it posed the problem of how we do develop our tools for thinking, and that this could only happen if we were able to use that electricity, that potential difference which arises from a series of oscillations between differing points of view. Among these I would emphasise:

- The links we have between the unconscious and dreams. We can observe this in both directions: the dream as the path, the key for reaching the unconscious, but also the dream that continually creates the unconscious through the work of the *dreaming ensemble*;
- The links we have between field theory, strong relational theories, enactment, and self-disclosure, and the need for boundaries against an excess of subjectivity;
- The links between our history with its deep roots and our need of a future: being proud of what we have discovered, being astonished at the new worlds that our instruments continually open up;
- The links between a point of view that focuses on contents, history, childhood, and sexuality and another which focuses on work to expand our repertoire of tools for "dreaming unthought dreams", for transformations in dream, and for living the session like a dream – from beta to alpha: dreaming

the analysis, considering sexuality as an indicator of the relationality between minds.

In these oscillations we create that vital electricity which is necessary for moving forward, developing new theories on the shoulders of our ancestors. The more we know, the more we have to discover and construct: (in four words) how to alphabetise O.

From O to K: the oneiric column of the lie

Manuela is ten-year-old girl in analysis. She is ultra-compliant, in competition with her sister aged twelve who has recently recovered from a serious illness, because of which the parents have granted her wish to have a German Shepherd puppy.

Manuela's analyst is very disturbed by what he considers an imprudent acquisition, an intrusion into his analysis of Manuela who has a "phobia about dogs". He decides to talk to the parents and rebuke them for thoughtlessly disturbing Manuela's analysis, and so on.

What Manuela's analyst does is leave "a fact" (the purchase of the puppy) as just "a fact" – or rather, an O within the therapy – without directing this O towards its subjectivation within the analysis itself: that is, allowing a move towards meaning, from "fact in itself" – from beta elements, if we like – into K, alpha, narrative.

In other words, if we are in analysis, any O can only follow the path of column 2 (yes, that of lies), in order to be transformed into the subjective truth of that analysis which is nevertheless a twist/ travesty/ transformation of O (as Grotstein, 2007, constantly reminds us).

At bottom the puppy could, from this perspective, be dreamed as the hooligan Manuela is afraid of, as something alive and new which arrives inside the analysis and inside Manuela's psychic life, and the parents who make such a purchase can, from a certain point of view, be the dreamed description of the analyst's work, which has been able to bring something new and alive into the analysis.

This view of the possible subjectivation of O should have been the view taken by the analyst, who should have been fully prepared to receive the transformations of O.

Naturally, other vertices are necessary, but they are not so cogently psychoanalytic.

At bottom, the setting up of a transformative narration passes through the dreaming "of the facts", so that they can become narremes of a completed narrative. This involves having the courage to consider the dream not as a way of coming into contact with emotional or psychic truth, but as a lie capable of bending O to our needs for meanings and narratives which organise emotions, affects, contingencies

After the analyst has, for personal reasons, cancelled a week of sessions, a patient dreams of being burgled by his own son, whom he had always trusted and from whom he would never have expected such conduct.

If we want to proceed with this exercise, the "fact" is the cancellation of four sessions by the analyst: what is inserted into column 2 gives an origin to the dream; that someone whom the patient trusted has betrayed his trust by stealing something from him. In other words, "the fact"/cancelled session becomes "you, my analyst, have stolen something, and I didn't expect this. Can I go on trusting you?" Put still another way, the dream becomes the instrument for subjectivation of O, a lie which enables us to think, feel, and give meaning.

Circular time and linear time

A young psychiatrist aged 35 tells me about a depressed patient of hers and how she cannot find the reason for the depression. This basic premise is then diffracted through a series of characters, depressed patients seen in the psychiatric clinic where she works. Without interpreting these characters as aspects of the psychiatrist herself, I confine myself to allowing the conversation to develop with highly unsaturated interventions.

At the end of the session she tells me a dream her fiancé had when he slept at her house (a dream that I consider relevant to our analytic space – whoever had it): she was forcing him to travel to Paris, but showing him a dangerous and very awkward cliff path above the sea.

Then he found himself in a cube which was running along a pre-determined track, opening every now and then and stopping, before setting off again towards a new stop and then another. It was a journey he had to make, but without taking any pleasure in it.

The patient had herself commented, "But why does my fiancé think that living together would be precarious, dangerous – a nightmare even,[2] with predetermined stops, and nothing good about it?" In this way she gives voice to her own doubts about taking steps she does not feel ready for (living together, getting married, having children), because she had yet to experience true freedom – her free spaces were blocked up, and they scared her. And yet, the prospect of giving these up obviously made her quite depressed. Here too, the patient presented a gap between her "real" age and her chronological age.

A woman of 45 tells me at the first consultation that she is tormented by the fear that her children will become ill. Then she says that she has lived with this fear for nine years – that is, for nine years she has not been alive. Things started to go wrong when her second child was born. She is always there to catch any sign of a cold which might be the start of a fever, and then who knows what?

I tell her that she seems to feel as if her children were the ball and chain on a convict's ankle. Why wouldn't she sometimes feel the urge to get rid of them and escape from her life sentence?

"Absolutely! And I completely understand those mothers who kill their own children. Ever since they were born there's been no cinema or theatre, and no boyfriends."

I say, "You're finding yourself in the position of a duty doctor in a resuscitation unit." The conversation continues with the recognition that time stopped nine years ago: she is 45, but feels only 22 or 23.

I then say it's understandable that the deaths of her children (whom she loves) would allow her to leave her maximum-security prison, and she would be able to find a way to give a life to that part of herself that would like "to live recklessly, one of those lives where it's never too late".

She connects to this idea immediately, listing all the things she would like and which she thinks she must now give up forever!

Time stopped at the age of 23, and at the (mental) age of 23 she finds herself with the burden and responsibility of a family that only a woman in the fullness of her own adulthood could manage.

This is followed by a long account of her mother's illness, which seemed to have stopped time.

She talks about how she has always wanted to visit New York and would still like to, and I am able to tell her that all she has to do is call in at the travel agency to buy a ticket-analysis which will enable her to re-set her time zones and regain her lost time.

I have addressed this topic in a contribution to the book edited by Gabriele Junkers, *Die leere Couch. Der Abschied von der Arbeit als Psychoanalytiker*, which looks at the passing of time in the life of an analyst and the consequences it has. Among other things, in our article (Ferro, et al., 2013) we emphasised the marked tendency in some psychoanalytic institutions to infantilise the young (the candidates), an operation which at the same time enables training analysts to unburden themselves of 20 years (sometimes 30), giving everyone the illusion of circular time: going back to school for some, and finding the elixir of eternal youth for others.

When Valeria comes in for her session, I think, "I bet she's pregnant". Then she starts telling me that she has something extraordinary to say to me, but first she must tell me a dream: she was in a room where there was a worn-out sofa. She was happy because there was a new-born baby, but at the same time there was the baby's grandfather, now very old, and diagnosed with an illness which would shortly cause his death. Then she tells me the great news: she is pregnant! I don't know how it is possible that I had thought this as the patient came in for her session.

She recently turned 40, and has been in a satisfying relationship for a little while: the time was now ripe. In the same way, the time was now ripe for ending her analysis, a plan which had taken shape in the previous sessions: there is the baby of flesh and blood and there is the baby plan to "terminate the analysis". It is time for the analyst, now a grandfather, to get ready to leave the stage and to accept the linearity of time.

Loredana arrives talking about ending her own analysis in an entirely unconscious way where time seems to take the form of sequential steps in which everyone has found his proper place: at the age of ten, Manuela will finish primary school next year; Sandro, at 13 will finish middle school; and Salvatore will finish high school. In her own turn, she herself will have to leave her old job, which has nevertheless served her very well in enabling her to build up her professional skills, and she will start her own legal practice. Her husband will cut his ties with his father's firm, which he has been running, and will set up his own consultancy service. The only problem, says Loredana anxiously, is how to arrange things for her own widowed father. Some will have to take care of him, and maybe a good retirement home would be a solution for him. I tell her that everyone seems to have found their proper location (her child, adolescent, and adult aspects) and that her father, now a grandfather, must let them all be free to follow their own paths, withdrawing in turn to his own proper place.

In praise of lying

The lie is a way of creating worlds that may be more habitable.

It is common in science fiction stories, novels, or films that a spaceship from an uninhabitable world tries to reach Earth or, conversely, spaceships from an Earth that has run out of resources set off in search of new worlds.

The lie is often this spaceship or this new world with characteristics which make it habitable: that is, it is one of the many defences we can make use of in order to survive. We have infinite examples, starting with Ulysses, who tells Polyphemus to call him *No-man*, which will save him from the fury of the Cyclops when, blinded by Ulysses, he will ask his brothers for help and when they ask him who has blinded him he will answer, "No-man!"

Another famous example is the previously mentioned Bishop in *Les Miserables*, who saves Jean Valjean, who had stolen all his belongings, by lying to the gendarmes to protect him.

Bion fundamentally acknowledges the lie's value both through what is well known as the "Liar's Metaphor", and in his claim that the lie needs a thinker. That is, in certain respects – and paradoxically, the lie needs a creative thought: we can think of the worlds invented by someone having an extramarital relationship who needs to furnish with details the richest worlds which would not otherwise have existed.

The lie, or at least degrees of it, saves us from truths that are too unbearable to think about: that there is no life after this one, that we live in the most absolute randomness, that we no longer feel love for a person we have loved and now only feel fond of them, and so we should therefore leave them.

The lie and the compromise open up for us infinite ways of existing, ways fitted with shock absorbers. All the defence mechanisms are in the end only degrees of possible lies, where the truth, O, is not only unknowable, but also unbearable.

Therefore, I consider the capacity to lie as one of the signs of an achieved psychic maturity and also a sign (not the only one) of a possible end to the analysis.

It is obvious that I am not referring here to those who use lying as a way of life and for their own ends, but those who – in extreme (and sometimes chronic) emergencies and, I would add, with elegance – are able to tolerate this defence mechanism.

At bottom, every defence mechanism is a lie when set against an intolerable truth.

Notes

1 Translator's note: The analyst is playing on the name of the province Emilia-Romagna.
2 Translator's note: The fiancé dreams he is *"in un cubo"*. A nightmare in Italian is *"un incubo"*.

7

ON THE SUBJECT OF SUPERVISIONS

Group supervision

In my opinion, this is a very valuable tool in training. I tend to organise super-visions in such a way that the groups are "mixed", in the sense that young analysts can take part, bringing freshness and naiveté, alongside thoroughly trained analysts who bring experience and rigour, to their mutual benefit. I also bring together colleagues who work with adults, adolescents, and children, starting from the pre-supposition that the only differences between them will be terminological and that mental functioning is unitary (Ferro and Basile, 2009).

Every supervision group consists of six to eight participants who meet once a fortnight for an hour and a half. The group is open, in the sense that people join it when there is a vacancy and leave whenever they wish.

This last feature is fundamental, in my view, because the wish to take part must depend on the interest which the group arouses.

Clinical cases are presented in turn, taking the form of a brief history (roughly two pages) followed by a brief discussion; then written accounts (not recordings) of one or two sessions are read out. These accounts are written after the session has ended without notes being taken during it, so that there can be a first filtering or "sieving effect" which allows what is not necessary to flow away and keeps the parts that it may be helpful to communicate. This is followed by further discussion and elaboration by the group and finally by me.

This is the basic plan, which has been through a series of permutations. The first came when I realised that it could be useful to transcribe an adult session – leaving in the invariants – as if were a session with a child, and vice versa. Naturally, a dream could be replaced by a drawing and play, and so on. In this way, the con-fluences, the similarities in mental functioning become clear despite the diversity of language.

Choosing to see a unitary basic mental functioning in the genesis of symptoms (Ferro, 2002b), I came to add an exercise about the different ways in which a symptom can express itself and be expressed, if we set aside as invariant the fundamental problems (managed with different defences or in different modes). For example, a session with an obsessional engineer with Asperger's characteristics can be transformed into a session with a depressed woman who tends to somatise. In other words, the same betaloma (Barale and Ferro, 1992) could have found a different means of expression by choosing different symptoms and defences.

Naturally, group supervision does not permit a single case to be followed over a long period (because the presenter changes every time) but it does allow the introjection of a method, using the errors, doubts and, problems of the other participants in the group.

There are more and more participants from other countries and speaking other languages, sometimes regulars and sometimes occasional visitors, who have further enriched the working atmosphere and helped the group to get used to re-setting itself in response to unforeseen demands.

I have gone into more detail about these activities in the tutorials included as the concluding chapters of two of my books (Ferro, 2007; 2010) and before that – in connection with the various modes of supervision – in the collection of Seminars conducted in Brazil (Ferro, 2012).

Up until now this had been work on "contents". When the change of direction occurred (mine and others', especially Ogden and Grotstein), shifting from the prioritising of contents to the development of instruments for thinking, feeling, and dreaming (that is, the development of $\female/\male$ and alpha function), then new exercises came to life, I would say irresistibly and almost by themselves.

In fact, if the aim of analysis is to help the patient dream the dreams he or she has not been able to dream, it is precisely this oneiric/ transformative/ narrative function that must be developed.

So, we have had a new exercise: during the usual case presentation, some (very) brief phrases are selected (seven was the magic number agreed upon) which each participant would have to use to construct a different short story (using the same brief phrases with freely chosen additions).

In the end, this is what we do when addressing the patient's story: we select certain "loci" and assemble them, adding the missing pieces in order to form a coherent intervention.

What has been interesting in regard to these stories made by each participant (out of the same narremes) has been:

a   how profoundly different they could be from each other;
b   how there were some common invariants;
c   how there were certain prevalent narremes, ones that stood out and became foci, almost embryonic organisers of particular attention;
d   how all the stories had an increasing degree of inventiveness, freedom, and creativity.

We could say that the experiment had been successful and that this exercise, in addition to those described previously, had contributed to developing the meta-bolic-narrative ability of each participant in the group.

We could collaterally observe how there was a significant narrative coherence among the various stories and that there was hardly any intrusion by constructivist attempts to force excessive or arbitrary meaning on them once the narrative genre had been chosen.

This leads me naturally to reflect on the analyst's indispensable subjectivity (Renik, 1998), but also on the necessity of not doing violence to the text, of giving it coherence without abusing it. In terms of theory, we could say that this exercise is located in the capacity for expanding as far as possible the oscillation between selected facts and negative capability (Bion, 1970).

Naturally, all the different types of exercise can be made more complex through the introduction of a further variable: for example, that of choosing certain narrative genres in which to write the stories – science fiction, noir, detective thriller, war story, tragedy, comedy, and so on. There is no limit to the degree of complexity that is possible.

A further exercise, on a still more abstract and creative level, is simply to suggest "a title" to the members of the group (a topic chosen on the basis of something significant which had taken shape in the normal work of group supervision) and give them the task of writing a short story about it, using sometimes one narrative genre and sometimes another.

This last kind of exercise has revealed – or unveiled or activated – a creative capacity which individual members of the group had not hitherto been able to express, and narrative genres they had not previously been able to appreciate. Identifying this "lack of appreciation" enabled everyone to reflect on the less accessible areas of their own minds.

If we think that the meaning of a session, or of an analysis, could be defined as the patient's acquisition, through the work done with the analyst, of the ability to dream those dreams he or she had not been able to dream before (Ogden, 2007; Ferro, 2009) and of continuing this work once the analysis is over, this exercise performed upstream of the contents assumes obvious importance.

As I was suggesting, these kinds of exercise also allow each analyst to see which narrative genres he is fluent in and which are those he finds most diffi-cult or obscure. Such a discovery is in itself therapy if one has the patience to continue with these exercises.

In the end it is kind of exercise for film directors: someone who has a talent like Sam Peckinpah's or Quentin Tarantino's will find that he is directing his "films" too far in that direction and that he lacks the sensibility of a Tavernier or a Bergman, or the darkness of Buñuel. The analyst who stays closer to rea-lity, if "forced" to make up science fiction plots, will have to open herself up to a new type of listening and fantasying, just as the most imaginative will learn a lot from the "hard reality" of Rossellllini's *Germany Year Zero* (1948). These last exercises have been published in *Nel gioco analitico: lo sviluppo della creatività in psicoanalisi da Freud a Queneau* (Ferro, et al., 2015).

Individual supervision

As time passes I feel less and less that I am providing my supervisees with a model or method but trying to help them find their own ways of doing and understanding psychoanalysis. I am not interested in acquiring disciples but in helping each individual become a good analyst with his or her own talents and aptitudes.

I don't enjoy the first series of supervisions because it has to involve some element of West Point in the learning (or teaching) of good psychoanalytic conduct – often to excess, which is of little use in the field – but the introjection of the academy will nevertheless continue to be important and constructive.

I prefer working with candidates who have progressed further in their training or with colleagues who have been more "worked on". For years I have been receiving requests for supervision from training analysts all over the world, and I conduct these supervisions with the greatest interest because I learn so much from different ways of working, the fruit of years of experience.

Even so, there are some specific dance steps which I tend to suggest (and which the supervisee is naturally free to adopt or not):

- Always considering the patient's responses to interpretation in a different way from other types of listening (Faimberg, 1996; Joseph, 1985), even as a dream about the interpretation she or he has received.
- Considering this "response" as helping you to formulate the next interpretation (or rather, intervention), using the information received without necessarily making it explicit that you are doing so. (In terms of theory, I regard the "response" as a derived narrative of the waking dream sequence produced by the alpha function stimulated by the interpretation.) I therefore consider the patient as a GPS which enables a continuous interpretative modulation according to what the "response" tells us about the patient's alpha function and the functioning of $♀/♂$ – or, it would be truer to say, of the field in constant transformation.
- I listen to all the patient's communications as transference communications (these things he brings to me – and their diffraction in the field).
- Oscillation between saturated and unsaturated interpretations: in/of the transference and in/of the field.
- Differentiating work in the kitchen area of the analyst's mind from that of the restaurant area (where the food is served, the interpretative intervention offered).
- Avoidance of commonplaces and interpretations "by the book": those which two different analysts could give if we imagined them being in the same session.
- Dreaming the session and the sequences of sessions.

But I think the best we can hope for from the work of supervision may be not to "train a string of parakeets" (Nissim Momigliano and Robutti, 1992) but to spark a love for the new, a curiosity about what we don't know, and a readiness to navigate without too many charts, apart from the basic ones (negative capability, tolerance of frustration, acceptance of pain and joy, the ability to change and to develop oneiric functions, and quite a few others); for all these aspects see Ferro et al. (2007) and Gaburri (1997).

I realise I often slip from a relational model to a field model, but I too am on a journey towards a pure field model (in analysis we only dream new things that are waiting for a new field to come to life): but it would be too complicated for me and for the reader to maintain this strong vertex as the only one. This is true even though, from a theoretical viewpoint, I tend to explore the horizons of the pure field.

I think that these (and other) ways of challenging the dreaming ensemble may be useful in developing our (analyst's and patient's) dream-functions.

Larry Brown and Carol Tarantelli recently (2011) made some astute and pains-taking reflections about Bion's discovery of the alpha function which inaugurated the new study of dreaming beyond the limits of dreaming at night.

It should be remembered that, when Bion was in analysis with Klein she had, from his point of view, misunderstood his assertion, "Oh yes, I died on 8 August 1918!" (the day of the battle of Amiens in which Bion had taken part) since she had taken it to be a metaphorical statement, whereas he felt that it had been an impossible experience to metabolise: I would add, until that moment.

But are we here setting ourselves the problem of trauma? Does it only consist in its tragic and undigestible reality, or also in the insufficiency of rêverie with which it was experienced and in the lack of alpha function with which one had to deal.

This would open the way to a different therapy of trauma which would also consist in the development of the dreaming ensemble I have talked about so often before.

What wounds of the soul can be healed? Are some wounds impossible to heal? Can this perhaps be addressed by the development of tools for dreaming? Under the influence of "one's own battle of Amiens", is it there that one's own alpha function is discovered, activated, and challenged? But couldn't we reverse this viewpoint and imagine the entire narrative of the battle of Amiens as if Bion had tried to narrate the collapse of the non-psychotic part of his personality when it was overwhelmed by the psychotic part, using the literary genre of war fiction to describe it. This could occur when beta elements overload and destroy all the containers and every residue of alpha function, leading to a catastrophe for the psyche. But what is the battle of Amiens? Could it be one of the possible terrible experiences which sometimes happen in our lives? Could we think that under the fire of beta elements we can either evacuate them or activate instruments for transforming them into alpha?

In this case, Bion – using, as I said, the genre of war fiction – might have been able to narrate the experience which if treated differently could have led to a psychotic crisis.

This kind of experience could have been narrated in different genres. The only opportunity we have for engaging with these states, beside psychic death, is by activating a system capable of initiating the metabolization of this dreadful sensori-ality: attending therefore to the development of alpha function and to the "thinker" capable of thinking those thoughts which are in search of just such a thinker, or perhaps I should say dreamer.

I will now present some examples of exercises which help us to develop these abilities (Bertogna, 2014) and open up blocked passages, helping us to show in the flesh what I meant in describing them.

Opening blocked passages: aka, the WD40 function

The title of this section is the task assigned to the group, followed by an example of each genre written by one participant, for the sake of brevity; in the book cited earlier (Ferro, et al., 2015) can be found all the exercises and responses from all (or almost all) the members of the group.

1. I'm not the first today

Permutations via the genres of detective thriller, romance and film noir.

Detective thriller – the serpent knight

He noticed the "No entry" sign, but ignored it and went inside. I'm not the first today, he thought to himself with some bitterness, and then he saw her. She was lying on the floor with a sad expression on her face as if she was asleep, submerged in the sleep of a discontent with a life where there was no homeland and no past. For a moment he thought she was dead. He leaned over her and realised that her heart was still beating. He tensed as a sudden noise broke the silence.

I'm not alone in here, he said to himself, I'd better get out of here fast. He looked around and tried to find an escape route, but the door opened.

"Congratulations, Inspector, you finally got here."

He recognised the Cobra straightaway. He'd got his name from his insane passion for the snakes he kept in his house. Here he was, the serial killer he'd been hunting for so many years. He saw the gun and only after that noticed the open tank, and the snakes that were swarming out of it …

I'm trapped, he thought, paralysed by fear …

The woman moved, half opened her eyes and needed no more than a glance to see what was happening. "Look out!" she shouted as a cobra lunged towards him …

"Inspector, Inspector, wake up … your shift is over … how did it go with the Cobra?"

It was the sergeant coming on duty. He opened his eyes. He felt strangely rested. He had succeeded in catching the Cobra.

Romance – the laundry

This is the story of an enchantment.

Linda had spent her entire life like a child looking out through the glass door of a washing machine, always ready to wipe away and get rid of any trace of life.

She had met Bruno by chance one evening on TV, in *The Barbarian Invasions*. His view of himself had always been "I'm not the first today … it's always the same." He seemed a strange barbarian, in fact a gentle barbarian, kidnapped and held prisoner in the jungle by the Maoists.

She had heard him speak and fallen in love with him, listening to his story when, despite being bound and gagged, he had turned his face up to the Moon and the stars and had felt a moment of happiness.

This is my man, thought Linda, and loved him at the mouth of the Po, among mud and mosquitoes.

Film noir – clan-destiny

Everyone knows me as the man with no reverse gear, because I don't give a damn about anybody. I've got my followers and they're afraid of me. They call me a monster, but it's just that I put myself first. The sooner you understand that life's an ugly business, the better. I've lived in the slums, among thieves, murderers, and whores, people like me. All it takes is one look and we understand each other. Talking is for cops and spies. Like Samantha, that bitch who squealed and got me sent to jail. I've been waiting a long time for her. I know she'll come one day, I'm in no hurry. My revenge needs me to go all the way.

I'm not the first today…. What the fuck's going on? There's too much movement here in the harbour…. I need to call Vito. But wait a minute … that's … yes, that's Samantha…. Look how she's changed, all dressed up like a fine lady … but now, my darling, just come over here so I can blow you away….

"Hello, Samantha … remember me?"

I can read the panic in her eyes. Dumb. So you know how to keep quiet now, do you? I just have to drag her into the alleyway, plunge the knife into her chest, feel the blade penetrate her flesh and tear it, and then … then, nothing. I'm swallowed up in the darkness of the night. I've got to get home…. I've got to find something to live on…. Fuck, what's that line of poetry by whatshisname? "When you look at the sea, happiness is a simple idea …"

2. He cracked his knuckles

Permutations via the genres of science fiction, comedy, and history.

Science fiction – hand crafted

There is life on Mars. He had always known it, ever since that Tuesday when he'd heard that troubling music, like someone cracking their knuckles. Where does that melody come from?

And he'd known the Hands. They had appeared out of the book, beautiful, slender, well-manicured, and had pointed to those few lines: "Retrace your route and stay suspended in the limbo of free intelligence. You must construct a barrier against the dictatorship of facts."

He cracked his knuckles, to feel that music again, and looked thoughtfully at the horizon. In the distance, the light of the Earth was going out.

Comedy – the best friend

Professor Pierotti was a solid, stocky figure with an objective approach to life, no loose ends, nothing overdone, the greatest respect for rules and institutions. His only quirk was connected to the figure of his friend, Perozzi, a good-humoured joker who had emigrated years ago to Australia. To keep in touch with him, the Professor had taken to going to the bar every morning, the one near his school, and ordering two coffees: "One for me and one for my friend Perozzi," he told the barman. But one day he turned up looking awful. You could see at once that he wasn't well.

"Just one coffee today ..." he said in a low voice.

"What's wrong, Professor. Is your friend ill?" asked the barman in some surprise.

The Professor cracked his knuckles and answered, "No, no ... he's fine ... it's just that I can't drink coffee anymore."

History – a snapshot from Berlin

For as long as he could remember, he had always lived in the forest. He slept in a damp, dark cave, fed on what nature provided – he loved maize – ate the animals he hunted and the fish he caught with his rod – that was a lot of fun – he moved along the rivers in his canoe carved from a tree trunk and warmed himself by his fire. Tuwonga, his dearest friend, had one day shown him that strange clay paste, dipped his hands in it and made prints of them on the walls of his cave. How they made it shine! He had cracked his knuckles with excitement.

So many boys and men have left their handprints over the years ... we can see some of them on fragments of the Berlin wall.

3. Seven underlined phrases

- nights out
- a knife in the back
- found beaten to a pulp
- go home and sleep
- electric collar
- this strange room
- she was jealous

Permutations: horror, sentimental, porn.

Horror – Paradise Lost

Adam was not used to nights out. He had always lived in the institution, a warm nest that kept him safe from a world of dangers. But that day the director had sent for him and told him that he could leave next month. He felt a knife in his back. "They want to get rid of me!"

He let his eyes fall on the newspaper lying nearby. The headline was a message: "Man found beaten to a pulp."

"That's what they want to happen to me!"

He had stopped and gone to look out of the window at the agitated toing and froing of the people who thronged the street and the park at that time of day.

"They're all going home to sleep," he thought, "without knowing he's been killed ... filthy bastards!"

A woman was walking with her white poodle on a lead, but looking at it more closely he realised that it was an electric collar.

"I could use it on the Director, that electric collar. She's got white hair too.... It seems very obedient to its mistress ..."

He turned to look at this strange room. A heavy metal paperweight was lying within reach of his hand.

"I've got to get rid of her first ... she was jealous of me.... Those eyes!"

"Adam, I meant to tell you that your mother is waiting for you downstairs ..." the Director whispered nervously. A strange feeling of danger had taken hold of her.

Adam picked up the paperweight, aimed it at her heart and struck her with all her strength: "I was right to kill her, she is Satan."

Sentimental – in the shell

Elisa always looked forward to her nights out with Carlo. It was as if she had always known him and even had conversations with him in her dreams. The news that he was going away had come violently, without warning, like a knife in her back. His boss was sending him abroad because a man had been found dead, beaten to a pulp.

"Now everyone's going home to sleep, while I have pack a suitcase and leave," Carlo had said to her, not without a certain sadness.

"Don't tire yourself out," Elisa had replied, looking at the lime tree where they had often met, trying to find a bit of consolation and not feel abandoned. Pain can be like an electric collar for a dog, it tames you. And leaves a mark.

"In this strange room that's our relationship," thought Elisa, "I never thought he could open the door and walk out." She was jealous, and surprised at herself for the first time.

Porn – the gust of wind

Romeo knew he had a real treasure in his pants. All his dick needed was two strokes and up it went.

"This is where I get my ideas from.... How many I've had.... And besides, I've always liked pussy," he thought with satisfaction.

Maria was an attractive forty-year-old who knew how to enjoy life and, on the advice of her gynaecologist had given up wearing knickers.

They met when a mischievous gust of wind shamelessly lifted up Maria's dress ...

"Well.... This could be a very tasty evening!" said Romeo to himself.

On his nights out he felt like a stallion. But the other evening, the frosty gaze of that tease had hit him like a knife in the back. He'd rather have been found beaten to a pulp. Romeo felt like he'd lost his way. He looked around the strange specimens of humanity who populated the members' only club and thought, "Now they're going home to sleep ... but as for her over there, I'd put an electric collar on her and make her dance.... I never forgive ..."

But now destiny seemed to offer him a second chance: "I could do a bit of introspection with that lady. She looks easy enough to let me give her one on our first date." Without her knickers on, Maria felt free to fuck far and wide, and after all, she wasn't jealous.

Romeo went over to Maria, started chatting her up, and took her into this strange room, ready to make her experience that old pagan art they both knew so well.

In sex, as in life, he followed no script, but knew that a few pinches of her backside, a bit of licking, and a few thrusts up against the wall are enough to help living creatures like us drive away the thought of death.

He opened her legs and went deep into her dark forest.

It seems to me that exercises like these give a good flavour of the work we do, though you need to imagine this work being multiplied by the number of participants in the group, their shared reading, and the new associations which the group makes with them. No interpretation is made of these stories, neither individually nor in the functioning of the group. Their only purpose is the pleasure of seeing the development of the tools for thinking in the individual and the group.

Classic exercises are those of the kind which have appeared in my most recent books:

1. Patient: "I ate lamb today, and my daughter ate it too ..."
2. Which of these responses would seem to you most appropriate, and why? Which implied model could each one apply to, and why?

   a Longeque inferior stabat agnus
   b Like Montalbano we could say that the two of you were hungry as wolves
   c Your daughter is also getting ready for a career as a wolf
   d But I don't eat leaves
   e You are telling me that you have succeeded in not inhibiting the instinctual and voracious part of yourself

3. Patient: "I'm going to travel to China this summer, and I especially want to go to Shanghai: I'll travel in a lot of short stages."

a   It must be an exploration of an unknown world, one to enjoy

b   Small moves so that not too many emotions are stirred up

c   You're telling me that you are going to discover a part of yourself you've never passed through

d   Perhaps you're telling me you'd be risking an earthquake if you didn't exercise the caution that Shanghai requires

e   Could this be the way to get in touch with "Chiang Kai-Shek"?

4.   What models does the analyst have in mind? What is the inexplicit interpretation in certain examples, and why?

5.   What underlies or masks these interventions, or makes them explicit?

6.   A patient indicates that he "feels the need for us to see each other more often" and then brings a dream in which a bed salesman appears who tells his own analyst that he wants more women.

7.   The analyst interprets this by saying it seems obvious to her that the patient wants more sessions (see each other more often, another bed, adding sessions/meetings with the analyst).

8.   From what other vertices could this communication have been seen?

8

THEORISING THROUGH PRACTICE

In my opinion, it would be useful if we could always start with clinical work and move from there towards greater levels of abstraction: like Bion we could call it working our way from rows 1 and 2 of the Grid towards the top. Working in the opposite direction makes me think of travellers who keep their noses stuck in a guide book and miss discoveries and changes, anything that hasn't yet been mapped.

Dreams and their capacity for poetic syncretisation: the "derelict" house and the eyesore

Arianna tells me how terrible she finds the idea of having to face separations, bereavements, and losses in life just when she is building a stable relationship with a boyfriend and as the first signs are appearing of an end to the analysis.

She brings three dreams to the next session: in the first she has passed an exam but lost her certificate, which means she may have to retake the exam, whereas her classmates have had their passes recorded.

In the second dream, three obviously mafioso Sicilians come into her mother-in-law's tobacconist shop, claiming that she still has to pay protection money.

In the third, there is a three-storied house, inhabited but completely "derelict", its frontage unfinished and a lot of touching up needed. Next door is an enormous eyesore, built without planning permission and incomplete. There is also a cave filled with ceramic toilets, piled up in a heap but beautiful.

Before telling me the dream she says her boyfriend's father has been diagnosed with a tumour and given an uncertain prognosis, and she realises she's been talking to her colleagues in the hospital about her boyfriend's father and mother as if they were already her in-laws.

So the analysis has a finishing date. An internal set of links has now been constructed. There is the problem of bereavement and how to face separations, including the end of the analysis.

There is a fear that the patient will get no recognition of the time she has spent in analysis, just as the analyst (with the three sessions) does not want to give up his protection money. Looking ahead, the analysis is only a "derelict house", but to go on with it would defile the landscape and construct an illegal eyesore, although there is an awareness that other "sessions", other toilets, would need to be installed and used: but if we were to do that, the analysis would never end.

Evacuations

From the model described throughout this book and in detail in Ferro et al. (2013), the problem of evacuation becomes clear, occurring on several levels, among which I would like once again to focus on

- the hallucinatory level;
- the level of oneiric flashes.

The first is like a hurricane which causes a massive flood, a tidal wave filled with pieces of boats, pieces of houses, pieces of trees: all meaning is overwhelmed and fragmented. Fragments of "dream thought" and functions, and bits of apparatus are forcibly evacuated.

The second corresponds to a powerful storm which has also caused a deluge, but a more limited one: some dykes have broken and discrete fragments of "dream thought" have been evacuated, maintaining a possible meaning.

Naturally these phenomena can apply to all the sense organs, and so we would come across hallucinations and oneiric flashes that are

- visual
- auditory
- gustatory
- kinaesthetic
- olfactory.

Naturally, in this model we could have evacuative "rivals" such as tics or phenomena like enuresis or the various forms of incontinence that can be manifested, involving different modes of expression which are more "contained" in their choice of symptomatic manifestation. It is also true that characteropathic evacuations have a quality not very unlike the modes described above, and that a panic attack also represents an evacuative, though localised, mode.

It may be helpful to devote a few words to transformations in hallucinosis: in these we have an evacuative projection intermediate between hallucinations and oneiric flashes, after which what has been projected is taken back again, appearing capable of having a meaning of its own, one which makes itself felt by its very obviousness.

At this point we can no longer evade the problem of delirium and how it is constituted.

a   First of all, the channels linked to our senses are not to the fore.
b   There is usually a marked tendency to create links between facts which appear similar but are not connected.
c   There is considerable evacuation of proto-emotional states, often involving the projection of relatively fixed pre-configurations (pre-*fabulae*). For example, a pre-*fabula* could be the proto-emotion of jealousy + exclusion + coming into the background. This "Gestalt" could be put to work and "forced" to explain situations that are in themselves neutral.
d   Very often there are extreme attempts to give meaning to realities that do not have any meaning for the subject, or else they could paradoxically be related to many forms of dyslexia which arise from the experience of partially inde-cipherable emotions as a total enigma. The enigma of reading the world, the emotional world, the world of the other, and one's own inner world, has some roots in common with this other kind of enigma, albeit differing in intensity, profundity, extension, and degree.

Sexual disturbances

These can be understood as such (let's say from the perspective of how psychoso-matic disturbances are understood in general), or else as ways of conveying a pro-blem relating to mental functioning.

A sexual symptom is also a "character" who can be viewed along the three axes on which each character can be considered.

Fabio's disturbance

Fabio arrives with a problem of "erectile dysfunction": "he can't maintain his erection after penetration". Then he tells me about the "obsessive ruminating" he does about his relations with his family. He is always accommodating and incapable of bearing conflicts, never gets angry, and is terribly jealous but hides it from everyone.

Speaking about his last sexual encounter with his girlfriend, he says, "I'm ener-getic, I enter her, and then I relax completely, I go limp." He seems to be saying he isn't able to "go into battle" with his emotions. He is terrified, he adds, at the very idea of getting angry. Being unable to endure anger, jealousy, conflict, he cannot maintain his erect stance, he goes limp, he complies.

It is clear that behind the terror of conflict there is the terror of emotions too great to be managed, contained. There is a Jack the Ripper and an Othello who need the air taken out of them so that they'll go limp because he is afraid that they are uncontrollable.

The focus of interest clearly shifts towards Fabio's need for relationships without friction, relationships in which, in his own way, he gives up having an identity.

This is the nub of the analysis. It is possible that if Fabio acquires the ability to manage, contain and alphabetise his own emotions and is no longer afraid of friction and conflict, this may have other positive effects "on the symptom", a symptom which is nevertheless a narrative derivative of his waking dream-thought which – in all probability – has used this particular narrative to pictograph his need for an absence of emotions activated by conflict, the kind which occur in every relationship.

We could say that a problem like Fabio's could have been expressed through other symptoms of this kind, such as becoming strictly vegetarian or phobic about knives.

Symptoms, then, are not only "characters" of the session and narrative derivatives of waking dream-thought, but – viewed through the unitary lens of mental functioning as a whole – interchangeable, replaceable. One can take the place of another and have a very similar narrative and derivational meaning.

In the case I described we are confronted with a pathology of the container (incontinence ↔ hypercontinence) which could have found expression in enuresis or in sudden outbursts of rage.

Sexuality in the session

There are models which pay great attention to possible concrete sexual meanings in the session. Today – while it certainly meant something in the past – I find all this stale, defensive, and untrue. On the one hand, it reminds me of that sort of play on words lying in ambush for adolescents, and the formation of a code which later becomes fixed and decipherable. It is often a question of sexualised contents acting as antidepressants in the mind of the analyst.

A well-known French analyst writes that a patient who tells him she has forgotten to pay his fee and will bring it next time, should be interpreted as saying, "I'd like to pay in kind". I think this would not be the best way to ignite an erotic transference: in my opinion, we are more concerned today with sexuality between minds and how possible it may be to have a good (and equal) coupling of projective identifications and rêverie.

Listening to the patient and the magic filter

What a patient says in the session can be listened to through the filter which says "I had a dream". This helps us to deconstruct, de-concretise, and reorganise the communication.

Hepatic colic

On Monday morning a patient starts by telling me that his wife had an attack of hepatic colic which had to be treated with an injection of Buscopan and Voltaren, and then tells me about certain resentful acquaintances getting their revenge for wrongs done to them in the past, and then adds that he wished they would be more constructive. Listening to him through the "filter" ("I dreamed that my wife …") would lead me to think that the patient is talking about the pain of the weekend and of the approaching Christmas holidays, and that the Voltaren and Buscopan are his anger, his resentment that in some way cover his pain, and that the patient feels that a different attitude would be more constructive.

Luigi's bike

If – before the Easter holidays, during which he will miss two sessions – another patient, Luigi, tells me how nice it would be to go out on his bike in this lovely weather, and how he is planning to go out on his motorbike, like when he was a child and then a teenager, and his parents had given him a bike and then a scooter, and adds how wonderful it was to feel the wind in his hair, but that he also remembers a disturbing thought that has wormed its way in – which is that his parents had given him the bike and scooter "because they weren't interested in me, so that they didn't have to be with me" – then the interpolation of the filter would lead me to think as follows: for example – the holidays give him a sense of freedom, but from another point of view he is afraid that the analyst may take away his wheels-sessions (transforming his four-wheeled sessions into the two wheels of the bike and scooter) because of his lack of interest.

And what he then adds about the film *The Easy Life* [1] becomes the excitatory, manic equivalent of the previous patient's Buscopan/Voltaren. The car race, the excitatory antidepressant risk.

In my opinion, none of this should be decoded because we would risk turning it into a simultaneous translation. It should be kept in mind and cooked later on for serving to the patient in ways and doses that he or she can take in without needing to deny them.

In other words, from a certain point of view, every communication from the patient can only be about the analysis, and if we perform the operation of listening by means of our "transformation in dream" then every detail will appear significant for analysis, as is the case with a dream.

Voltaren, renal colics, riding on two wheels and so on, will be communications within the analysis, richly significant beyond their overt significance.

Stella and the Tamagotchi

Stella comes to analysis because of total alopecia. She then tells me about having been at the "German school" where it was impossible to show any kind of emotion if you didn't want the SS teachers after you.

She has occasional outbreaks of anger, rages about which she remembers nothing afterwards.

Over the course of the work it is possible to construct a certain repetitive functioning: a sort of depilation of the gorilla she periodically turns into – but the gorilla seems to jump out when the Other (whoever that may be at the time) does not answer the needs which Stella has but does not express.

At this point, her dream about the Tamagotchi becomes crucial: if the Tamagotchi is not cared for as it needs to be, it could just die, but it saves itself through outbursts of fury and "gorillification".

After years she finds a boyfriend-analyst who films her with a video-camera during her moments of fury, telling her, "I love you because you are my soulmate; I hate you because you are a beast." And so the split-off aspects can find a way of being brought together and put into the same film through the continuity of the analyst-cameraman's eye.

But this aspect of the need for integration of split-off and/or denied aspects is often the starting point for many analyses.

Caterina and Lucy

A patient, Caterina, is a devout Catholic and an excellent wife and mother but needs several defence mechanisms to manage "Lucy", her rebellious sister (part of herself), resorting to symptoms of anorexia-bulimia, vomiting-exorcism, and so on. Until she falls victim to the (split-off) "sister" and jumps over the wall in order to have orgiastic experiences of all kinds – partly as an antidepressant for a depression which has always gone unacknowledged.

Roberto and the wild boar

Roberto had been in psychotherapy about twenty years previously with the same psychoanalyst he comes to see again.

At that time, he had fallen into despair on finding that he was gay, which had caused a painful separation from his then girlfriend. He had two jobs: he was a metalworker in blast furnaces and studied violin at the Conservatory.

He forms a strong bond with Alessandro, with whom he lives making ever more aesthetically oriented choices, playing the violin, going to La Scala, associating with musicians and singers, giving up his rough job as a metalworker with its rage and fieriness which has sometimes led him into violent behaviour.

The aestheticizing aspect and the company of homosexuals seem to have wrapped up the tulle of a tutu around his more primitive, "raw" passions. But after 20 years of tranquil and idealised life, what has led him to ask for a new analysis?

They have taken on Jolanda as an employee at their alternative herbal therapy centre. She is an open-hearted and curvaceous young woman to whom Roberto feels terribly attracted, even though she is "a real country bumpkin" who thinks that Bach is a deodorant. He had thought his ideal woman was Audrey Hepburn, but how can he match her with this force of nature who has arrived in the shop?

It is clear that the split-off and denied "blast furnace worker" has violently reappeared on the scene: a wild boar had been transformed into a pink little piggy but now, after 20 years, a wild sow has also made her appearance, and he can't resist her passionate nature, nor does he want to.

Perhaps we can allow ourselves some open reflections on this particular type of psychic homosexuality which seems to be playing the role of "blocking and hiding".

This is a successful operation, except that the hyper-contents have come back after twenty years to knock on the door with all the outrageousness of a hurricane.

Lorella and the precipice

On her return from holiday, and more precisely during the last (fourth) session of the week, Lorella talks about a little road which she had to walk along in the mountains, between the meadow below and the one above.

A frightening little road on the edge of a cliff, but fortunately there was an iron handrail she could hold on to.

I lightly remark that the "iron handrail" has kept her safe from falling down.

She catches the pun[2] and immediately tells me about her friend Lorella (who has the same name) who has been badly injured in the heel by an iron tent peg which her boyfriend had left with the point sticking out.

This has caused a recurring infection with repeated operations and an intermittent fever.

I tell her that "rusty pieces of iron" sometimes play tricks like these, and ask her the name of this friend: "Stop making fun of me," Lorella replies, "You know very well she's got the same name as me!"

The relative normality to which we can aspire can be likened to a fruit salad of defences; they should/can all be present to a small degree and in a flexible way, and linked together by their ability to cope with the current emotional situation. We often diverge from this normality when one (or more) of these defence mechanisms becomes predominant or takes over completely.

Irina's snakes

Irina is a thoroughly socialised child brought to therapy because of a sudden attack of alopecia. Her mother is a "perfect" mother, and Irina is entirely compliant and obedient. Her only cross is her sister Irene, a thunderstorm of jealousy and aggression, who bullies her violently.

It seems immediately obvious that Irene also stands for a split-off part of Irena, a primitive part which Irina is trying to de-gorillify: violent emotions are shaved off the same way as her hair falls out. Irene could be thought of as a Medusa's head stripped of all the snakes/proto-emotions which sprout from it.

This is how I have tried to portray Irina/Irene's two modes of mental functioning, while also thinking that Irina stood for "little anger"[3] and that Irene was the name of a hurricane which recently battered the United States (Figure 8.1).

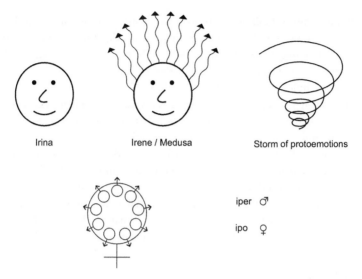

Irina   Irene / Medusa   Storm of protoemotions

iper ♂

ipo ♀

FIGURE 8.1 Irina/Irene's mental functioning

In a session Irina makes the following drawing (Figure 8.2), which we may be able to dream in a different way, so that we can find the killer she had told me about in a session.

The drawing consists of a montage of the same "pieces". The tonsure-negation defence can in this way be dreamed and can open a different story.

Laura and denial

Returning after the summer holidays, Laura talks about her two daughters aged five and 12, each of them suffering difficulties associated with the remoteness of their father. They have been angry with him, jealous of the other people he has

FIGURE 8.2 Irina's drawing

been with, and full of boiling emotions. Then Laura talks about her husband who denies all his emotions and even refuses to acknowledge the existence of emotion, and when Laura suggests that they should at least take the younger girl to the "psychologist", he is against it, telling her that he has no faith at all in psychology, except that psychologists can influence one's mind.

It is clear what is happening: in certain ways Laura is full of affects, emotions, jealousies, and needs which have to do with her analysis and the summer break, while on the other hand all this is strongly denied.

How can I say all this to Laura without her instantly rejecting it? For some time I have been making use of a particular interpretative mode, which involves stating explicitly what I am thinking about the interpretation. "I'm setting myself a problem. There are some things I would like to tell you, but I know they would make you angry and that you'd deny them. So, what am I to do? What I would say would be …" This kind of interpretation can often be useful.

Liliana and abuse

Liliana dreams she is in a doctor's waiting room and sees a middle-aged woman come in carrying a syringe full of a liquid which makes people turn red. The woman would like to inject this liquid into a teenage girl who is also in the room, but Liliana is against this and fights the woman so that she is only able to inject half the phial.

Liliana suffers from attacks of embarrassment and shame which cause her a number of inhibitions. It seems she can now fight against the injection which causes blushing and embarrassment. I do not interpret this in such a way as to decode the dream, but comment on what is happening in it.

The next day she tells me about a relative who, although he is married to a very wealthy but rather uptight, inhibited young woman, has now met a "red hot" girl from the South with eyes full of passion. Liliana's relative does not know what to do: maybe he has fallen in love with this girl, but what would that do the harmony of family life? If I listen to this "story" as a dream, it seems to continue the dream from the previous day: if the teenager is not inhibited by injections of shame and embarrassment, she seems to become this "passionate girl from the South" capable of bringing emotions and passions into the field.

Without realising it, I am glad to welcome this "new character" who has been added to the cast list, and perhaps in what I say I allow my predilection for intensity of emotion to leak out, instead of the serenity which derives from the emotional tranquillity of a bland low-calorie diet.

The next day the patient seems to change the screenplay and talks about her daughter at high school, who wants to change schools because she has a teacher who would like her students to think exactly like her, and the girl cannot bear this, feeling it as an abuse and an oppression. At this moment I see I've fallen into the trap of a story brought on by an "external fact" which Liliana finds herself confronting, since I fail to realise that she is continuing our dream. Liliana is telling me about my wobble of the day before in favour of the girl from the South, and how my "preference" had been felt by her as an abuse and an oppression, instead of giving her time and freedom to adopt a position of her own.

Notes

1 Translator's note: Italian title *Il sorpasso*: literally, "overtaking".
2 Translator's note: iron is "ferro" in Italian.
3 Translator's note: Irina is imagined as the diminutive of "ira".

9

GRADIENTS OF ALPHABETISATION

Introduction

This chapter originated as a collection of observations about the style and modes of thought used by Bion in *Cogitations*. Thoughts *in nuce*, more elaborated thoughts, and thoughts which illuminate and vanish but can potentially be reorganised by the reader in a profitable way so that they can set off new thoughts in their turn. However, I want to start with some observations arising from the reading of a themed issue of *Inquiry* currently awaiting publication.

I greatly appreciated the connection which Gail Reed has made in it between André Green and me because it is by no means an easy connection to make. In a European context there could be no greater distance than between Green and me. He is as tied to a conceptualisation of the drives as I am to a strongly relational model (whatever this may mean in a post-Bion, post-field context).

But, in fact, having many times had the good fortune to be able to compare my way of addressing clinical material with Green's, we have always in this respect found the greatest harmony and closeness in our viewpoints: in other words, although our theoretical models are different, we have always found that our technique and our theory of technique are very close. I am also grateful to Reed for having identified where there could be consonances from a theoretical view-point: in particular, with respect to anxieties of intrusion and abandonment, even within any single session.

So, I would like to add some reflections to the points emphasised by Reed.

It is true that my model and my technique arose from work with patients suffering from severe pathologies (borderline and psychotic), and also with children, but I believe that these technical modalities can also be used with neurotic patients, at least if they want to reach and explore the deeper levels of the mind where we find clumps of severe pathology (psychotic, borderline, autistic clumps).

For all patients, I think that the aim of analysis, rather than working on insight, on healing splits, on repressions and historical reconstruction, is the development of tools for thinking (in other words, alpha function, ♀♂, negative capability ↔ selected fact).

I have often said that I am "a reformed Kleinian", meaning two things by this:

a   that in my opinion it remains an indispensable part of training to make a journey through Kleinian thought and technique;
b   you then need to be "cured" of it, especially with regard to the constant decoding of unconscious phantasies and a certain risk of "simultaneously translating" what the patient says.

If a patient says she switched from an "iron with a flex" to an "iron connected via wi-fi without a flex" and she only needs to stand it on its base every, five minutes for it to recharge/reheat almost immediately, this should not necessarily be interpreted – or not interpreted as a passage towards a certain growth of autonomy (from the flex to the five minutes of autonomous) – but could instead contain a large quantity of meanings not to be decoded but co-constructed with the patient.

Naturally, I make absolutely no reference in my present technique to "unconscious bodily phantasy", which I think has now disappeared from even the most Kleinian of techniques. Today I would say that meaning is not pre-constituted and in need of deciphering or interpreting, but that the meaning is entirely to be "constructed" with the patient.

The analyst's interventions find themselves oscillating between unsaturated (French psychoanalysis would associate them with interpretations *in* the transference) and saturated (that is, *of* the transference), always waiting for the validation which the patient may or may not be able to give, considering her not only "the best colleague" but also a GPS who always tells us where we are and where we're going.

Using a Bionian jargon, I would like to add once again that Bion's Truth, Fact, and O (or beta elements, sensoriality) are as such unknowable and must be introduced and worked on in column 2 of the Grid (the column of lies and dreaming) in order to be metabolised and transformed into such truth as can be borne by the patient's mind.

A point on which there is a certain difference between Ogden, Grotstein, Green and me (and I really owe all of them a great deal and feel very much in harmony with the thinking of each one) is the strong presence of the field, not understood in the Barangers' simplified way, but in a more complex way where the internal group-character of analyst and patient gives way in the consulting room to a group of presences, characters I call "affective holograms", which are the fruit of the transformation in dream of what has been said, done, and experienced in the minds of analyst and patient, and which form a kind of group-mind which de-concretises and de-realises the communications, transforming them into an oneiric scene which "lives in the consulting room" and leads to the development of tools for thinking (Bezoari and Ferro, 1999).

In a way it is as if Ogden's "analytic third" had been diluted into a dream narrative of the two minds' functioning as they form the cast of characters that is required in order to give life to the dream they need to take care of and – even before that – bring to life.

With regard to the Botella's extremely important concept of "figurability", I would say that in a way it refers to scraps of story (at the border of mental story) where the concept of rêverie refers to something that is concerned (predominantly) with the mind's current functioning.

With patients who have problems of conceptualisation or symbolisation, I think it is central not only for the analyst to effect "transformations in dream", but for the analytic field to do so too. Only these transformations in dream will enable deconcretisation and the development of each communication's oneiric and emotional quota.

A central point to be underlined is that "each utterance and each response" bring forwards the process of making psychological what had been a chaotic and meaningless content. As Grotstein says, what we can do is to transform our experience of the truth (O) into fiction, mitigating our perception of it: which brings me to reflect on the chapter "Transformations" from Grotstein's book *A Beam of Intense Darkness* (2007), and on the journey which every "fact" has to make in column 2 of the Grid in order to be alphabetised.

The chapter "Transformations" is among the richest and most complex, and deserves careful reading. It starts with the famous example of the "poppies" and addresses the theme of invariance. But what does the Transformation work on? The answer is obvious: but what is O? Here Grotstein helps us to a deep understanding that the answer is dual. On the one hand, O is a term for *noumeno*. O also seems to be a collective term for the *noumena*, the ideal forms, absolute Truth and ultimate Reality, at least starting from the internal world: that is, the unrepressed unconscious. The other aspects of O are the sensory stimuli of our emotional responses to our interactions with external (and internal) objects.

This leads us to reflect on the fact that those who mostly adopt the first of these hypotheses about the source of O, have a tendency to consider Bion a mystic. Those who prioritise the second hypothesis tend to think otherwise. It seems to me that Grotstein helps us to consider these two ways of looking at O as being in a necessary oscillation, as Bion himself does when he suggests that "somebody ... should, instead of writing a book called 'The Interpretation of Dreams', write a book called 'The Interpretation of Facts', translating them into dream language ... in order to get a two-way traffic" (Bion, 1978b).

This would bring us to the need to distinguish two categories of beta elements which I would be tempted to distinguish as beta 1 and beta 2. Beta 1 are "the unrepressed unconscious" and beta 2 are "the sense impressions of emotional meaning". The beta 2 would be transformed in the cycle towards alpha; the beta 1 in the cycle from pre-conceptions to realisations. The "food for the mind" is *deconstructed* into its elements and then *reconstructed* into elements more suitable for being absorbed.

The invariant in the "food for the mind" is the emotions and, in the final analysis, the "truth about the emotional relationships". This is the relationship for which the narrative derivatives (Ferro, 2006b) are variants, and what counts is the emotion that underlies these. The emotion becomes the more pregnant the more it exists within a link.

Grotstein (2009) writes that "'just as reason is emotion's slave' (Bion, 1965, p. 171) so the emotions are slaves to (containers of) truth. Thus, truth is the invariant, and emotion is its vehicle or container."

The continual re-dreaming performed in the field or, to put it more simply, by the patient who points out every "wrong turning" or the danger of submerged rocks, reminds us of the Conrad story, *The Secret Sharer*, mentioned earlier.

I shall take this opportunity to make a brief digression: if it is true that there is the utmost symmetry in the development and evolution of the field, it is equally true that the ethical responsibility for staying on course and maintaining the setting – that is, the ethical responsibility for a safe voyage – is asymmetrically born by the analyst.

Column 2, or rather, the journey through it, enables "facts" to be transformed into narratives, and people into characters. This is brought about by the dreaming ensemble made of the basic activities of rêverie, flash rêverie, short-film rêverie, transformations in dream, dreams, and talking as dreaming.

In particular, transformations of the patient's communications in dream (and equally their transformations in play) enable the continual provisioning which the field needs in order to survive and expand.

But the process of oneiricisation is yet more complex and less piecemeal, and concerns the whole session and the oneiric mode of travelling in it: the session becomes a dream produced by the two minds and is constantly regulated so as to permit narratives and transformations to take the place of the "not yet thinkable" or – in Ogden's words – so that it becomes possible to dream those dreams which, having not been dreamt before, gave rise to symptoms. But in order for this to happen, the field must become ill with the patient's illness which can only than be dreamed and transformed (Riolo, 1997).

Bion adds some brushstrokes to his theory of thinking: in particular he emphasises the importance of invention, of creating tools to think with. This is so that our mental capacity can bear steadily heavier tasks: above all, the development of the ability to think. Here, in my opinion, Bion gives us the keys to the most modern development of psychoanalysis: that is, passing from a psychoanalysis of contents, recollections, memories, to a psychoanalysis which looks to develop the individual's instruments and equipment for thinking, feeling, dreaming. Using Bion's terminology, we should at this point work on how to develop the capacity for alpha function, or how to foster the development of the container or of negative capability.

The analyst must be sensitive to the patient's unhappiness, always ensuring that it does not interfere too much with her ability to think. However, at the same time the analyst is in a dangerous situation, like an officer on the battlefield and with the attendant responsibilities. He finds himself also in the uncomfortable situation of being alone with his patient and – as I said earlier – depending on her as the best possible collaborator.

Thinking thoughts, living emotions, living the terror we can feel, taking upon ourselves the suffering of others, contacting the creativity in ourselves and in our patients, and letting it emerge, are perhaps good enough reasons for living, albeit in the full awareness of the insignificance of human existence. If, that is, we could accept the claim that we are a whim of nature, as Lucretius said, and if we were aware of the terror that this generates in us (and which is all the greater the more we deny it), then perhaps we might be able to do what the British and German troops did, as Bion reminds us, at the front on Christmas Day: play football in no man's land. If we could play with life's non-sense, maybe to the horror of all the high-ranking fundamentalists, would open up chinks of understanding and peace.

I constantly look to that Bion who has the courage to regard his own theorisations as transient and who is always in search of that wild, poetic, original something which a mind not too hidebound by false beliefs or false allegiances can generously create.

It is a sort of hymn to freedom of thought, a freedom which is the point of arrival at the end of a long journey from which we nevertheless need to free ourselves in order to be authentically free, as free as we possibly can be.

The transformation of People into Characters seems to me to be a fundamental step.

If a patient were to tell us about abuses or ill-treatment he had suffered, our listening should, in my opinion, tend in the direction of de-concretising, de-constructing, and as far as possible re-dreaming, as an instrument for reconstructing a narrative that may be different from (and more bearable than) the facts: for example, opening up a reflection on what the emotions are (however uncontainable they might be) by which the patient feels abused, and what type of relationship with the analyst or with other potential identities of the field determine this.

Dilution into narrative sequences enables previously undigested and indigestible "facts" to be become metabolizable.

It is perhaps worth remembering how there are two "*loci*" of creativity which lead to narrative: first, the way in which sensoriality is pictographed, forming mind-specific pictograms; and then the way in which these are later narrated in different narrative sequences.

It becomes evident that there is a difference between unconscious, shared – I might almost say, generic or "primal" – phantasies, and the sequences of pictograms which form the waking dream thought and are specific to each mind or to each analytic pair at work, or to each analytic field which comes to life.

The limit of the possible narrative derivatives and to the consequent opening up of the world is given by the announcements which continually come from the field, and in cases where the field itself is flooded or overflows, especially with the countertransference dreams which are kindled when the Maginot line of the field's boundaries gives way to emotional turbulences.

In this way, I look for a psychoanalysis concerned with the development of functions (for thinking, dreaming, and feeling) and not only a psychoanalysis which considers repressed or split-off facts (or emotions) (Nicolò, 2003).

Furthermore, rather than looking at the discovery or rediscovery of what has been buried or avoided, I look at the co-formation of new tools for thinking and to those future meanings which the field may be able to open up, also including the paradoxical transformative possibility of the memory of facts which never happened and are the precipitate of current experiences in the session, which are then post-dated during the session in après-coup.

It must be stressed that – however much the analyst may try to modulate the field – beta elements, sensoriality, facts undreamed by the patient enter it violently with no holds barred: the field is a great storehouse, hyper-receptive of turbulences that have yet to be alphabetised, with the complication that the analyst's subjectivity and her own turbulences (and defences against them) enter into the constitution of each couple-specific field (Riolo, 2007).

One paradox I would like to point out – returning for a moment to my way of doing supervisions – is that I try to develop the candidate's own attitudes and style, not to "bend" him to my convictions. To be entirely honest, I would be disappointed if a candidate ended supervision without having reflected on the news coming from the field (or the patient) and without considering the difference between the people and the characters of the session.

I think an analyst must have passed through and experienced various models (in particular, Freud, Klein, Bion) in order to achieve a distance from them and develop a personal creativity and points of view.

Bion used to say that there could be no Bionians because each analyst can only be himself, and I think I would be horrified to find myself faced with a "Ferrian" analyst, where I would be proud if she found some of my viewpoints useful and expressed them with others in her own way and not in imitation of me.

In my view, for an analysis to have meaning, there is nothing that does not have a place inside a consulting room and inside the oneiric field co-produced by patient and analyst in a functioning setting. Understood in this way, the field is more concerned with meanings to be generated, with the future, starting from the *hic et nunc*, with possible evolutions, including that of rewriting a different history.

Carlo and evacuation

Carlo is a homosexual patient who has been having panic attacks for some time and also suffering visual and auditory hallucinations. The images which occur to me as I hear his story are:

♂♂; ♂ ♂ ♀; – (negative) alpha function.

I use them to sum up the mental functions I am talking about:

- contents/contents with no possibility of containment;
- hyper-contents with a hypo-container, hence the panic attacks;
- inverted alpha function, hence the hallucinations.

Evacuation seems on various levels to be the prevailing mechanism of functioning. And what indeed would be more effective in the presence of a markedly inadequate (♀) or markedly occluded (♀●) container?

The hyper-betalomas (Barale and Ferro, 1992) can only be evacuated in hallucinations, in panic attacks, or crash into each other.

However, in all this Carlo has maintained some clumps of psychic functioning and capacity for dreaming: in one of these dreams of waste from the sink and the wc, a "quantity of dirty things" come out. This is exactly the description of the inverted functioning of one of the functions in the apparatus for thinking.

Potential criminality (delinquency)

Italo

Italo is a 50-year-old librarian separated from his wife. He has a marked stammer which causes him to alternate between relentless bursts of speech and sudden, unexpected stops. A sort of incontinence alternates with a hyper-continence which blocks him.

He says he would like to be "a man who makes an impact"

But this type of stammer (leaping ahead and abrupt stops) instantly express his relational modes.

He would like to start therapy straightaway, and arrives at the consulting room without an appointment, apart from re-introducing himself a year later.

And so a therapy begins, which is once again broken off, only to be restarted in a state of great urgency and need.

In one session he enquires of his therapist what he would do if a patient confessed to having killed someone, or even a lot of people.

He seems more and more to display two natures: the placid, slightly obsessive (hyper-controlling) librarian and the uncontainable Rottweiler, a breed of dog he says he is passionate about.

It seems to me that two such opposite tenants cannot live in the same apartment and that one of them must be got rid of.

As soon as the therapy has started, what had been intrapsychic enters his relationship with the therapist; after an effective interpretation, Italo replies that he has been to a Chinese restaurant where he ate "two toasts with shrimps" and then two little biscuits that were burnt.

He found the analyst's words anything but good (toast): they were not only "incomprehensible" (Chinese), but ashen (burnt biscuits).

In his dreams two ways of functioning appear, such as people with two heads or as pairs of twins.

Two ways of functioning alternate: Dr. Jekyll and Mr. Hyde.

But when can primitive structures, split-off parts, lead to an action? How does the transition from oneiric communication to "criminal act" come about? Could we also say "act against the intellectual capacities"? Act against the body?

I think all these situations have a highest common factor: that is, when the alexithymic, concrete aspect, the untransformed beta, undermines the container's capacity to contain and/or the alpha function's or dream's capacity for transformation.

When evacuation (into the body, into the body of society, into the intellect) undermines the mind's metabolic-digestive capacity for taking things in.

Whichever it is, I think the choice has a lot to do with existential contingencies and with the paths that have the steepest slope and seem best suited for evacuative discharge, whatever receptacle it may be that receives it. One receptacle may sometimes be sufficient, but at others it might be like Plitvice in Croatia, where one lake feeds into another and then into yet another.

These "lakes of beta elements" sometimes overflow the analytic couch and become real-life stories.

But although as therapists it is our job to work through a process of mourning, our transformative-containing power is nevertheless relative and limited.

At some point, the patient I was talking about will say he feels that analysis is like a chain (which perhaps binds or suffocates), but what will make a fierce Rottweiler more docile if not a chain in the hands of a sure master who knows how to restrain/contain it? In fact, the more the "chain" does its work, the more the patient will have dreams capable of portraying emotions that could only have been evacuated previously. "I met a girl in a brothel who seemed to be falling in love with me, and apart from fantasies about sexual violence, I think I could be falling in love with her too." We aren't very far from the plot of Ferrandino's *Pericle il Nero*. [1]

Disturbances in learning

With regard to disturbances in learning, I think there is an infinite number of causes, modes, and mechanisms upstream of the symptomatology itself: something that could in many cases be likened to the "operative thought" of psychosomatic illnesses (Ferro, et al., 2013). Perhaps we could speak of psycho-intellective pathologies in which the place of the soma is taken by the intellect, which becomes as it were embolised or micro-embolised by clots of beta elements. In many cases an inhibitory type of pathology is present, and in a great many others a "stupidification" as a defence mechanism against extremely violent emotions.

All defence mechanisms are useful for something: the problem is always their cost, the quantity of collateral effects that are incurred.

Socially too, and from a medical viewpoint, there is a progressive "scientifica-tion" of the emotional, finding organic pseudo-responses when the emotional and the mental are in play. These too could be thought of as legitimate and compre-hensible defences against the anxiety of knowing from other points of view, or of not knowing: but what is the cost of these defensive modalities? Besides, it is obvious that the "mind" is our species' most disturbing feature, along with the emotional – and perhaps it is all one thing. Saying that we suffer very little from it, or that it can investigated by means of the "emotional mental" is intolerable for many people; hence there is an abundance of pseudo-scientific explanations where description is exchanged for a cause.

Going back to the disturbances I was talking about, another frequent cause is the irruption of an archaic emotion, a real Hurricane Sandy (New York, 2012) which overwhelms the mental apparatus and can be "treated" with boredom, indifference, lethargy, stupidity, and it is no coincidence that there is a high level of intellectual performance in many cases of Asperger's syndrome (where the emotional is totally bonsaied and zipped up).

Velia

Velia is severely underachieving at school. There is nothing relevant in the diagnostic assessments. She is capable of an excellent rapport with animals – horses, dogs, cats, hamsters. Her ability to connect with her classmates and peers is steadily opening up.

At school she feels like, and calls herself, "a stupid cow". She can't understand anything, doesn't learn, can't memorise, and gets a string of low marks. Fortunately, she's a pretty girl which is some compensation for her. She starts psychotherapy because of difficulties in her relationship with her parents. Through a series of dreams, it immediately becomes clear that her world is one of loneliness, pain, and compressed emotions.

Although she poses as Marilyn Monroe, she is interested in finding her way in her emotional life.

After a year of therapy she has a dream, or rather a nightmare: it seems that thieves have broken in and ransacked everything.

The thieves seem to be the compressed and denied emotions which enter her mind and steal her peace and quiet: to Velia, emotions seem to be thieves of peace, so they must be rendered lethargic, switched off, except that this switches off all her curiosity, interest, ability to learn. When she tells me this dream, she talks for the first time about her sister Cristina, who does well at school and is very good at drawing. The dream's de-bonsaiing of the disturbing and therefore stupefied emotions opens up the appearance of another possible way of functioning: Cristina with her interests and abilities. A new world seems to open up when Pandora's box is gradually opened and when Velia is viewed in a different way, as someone who has potential that has never been expressed before.

Casting the characters

Eleonora starts Monday's session talking about how she hates her husband and how she wishes he'd die because he's "lazy, overbearing, and unpleasant". Then she recounts a dream in which she was "beating him almost to death". The therapist, seeing tears in the patient's eyes, hands her a paper handkerchief.

The patient goes on, talking about her daughter, Daria, who has "put on a few kilos and turned into a monster, so fat, covered in spots …"

Who are the main characters and how should we consider them? How does the "casting" happen?

One character is hatred, something extremely violent and uncontainable that she has inside her. Another character is "the husband" whom we could think of as the screen-character of the therapist, who is also hated for being lazy (he didn't work at the weekend). Then we have tears and finally the paper hanky (this character also stands for the ability to accept and "dry" the patient's unhappiness). After this operation of wiping away (the tears and the hatred) Daria appears: in other words, the way the patient sees herself as monstrous and hugely fat because she is "swollen with hatred" and pain.

The characters are "all" understood as functions of the field and are cast without any correspondence to external or historical reality: every character is a little vehicle, an excipient which conveys the "active principle" which needs to be expressed in the field at that moment (Petrella, 2011).

Thus, every patient contrives to find a character who corresponds to what he or the field need expressed.

But another character is the dream, through which the patient does not only tell us about content (anger and the desire for revenge).

Row C of the Grid

I realise that from the technical point of view, I work very close to row C of the Grid. I leave aside rows E and F (or perhaps I only use them as internal, personal, and provisional landmarks) in order to keep sharing level C (myths, dream thoughts, alpha sequences) as far as possible.

If a very inhibited, self-stupefied patient, talks about a catafalque, what I am spontaneously attracted to is the "falcon",[2] something extremely vital that is incorporated, locked away, asleep in the claustrum. I can't say this to the patient, but from that moment I will try to find a way of attuning myself to/with the "falcon".

In the same way, I am very much attracted by what I have called "semantic nests", sites of discourse which may enclose other, higher communicative possibilities. If, at a certain point, a hypothesis about abuse needs to be developed, the vertex from which I would position myself is: in what way may I have been abusive, or in what way may "the falcon" be (or have been) abusive? Moreover, that which belongs to another, external, historical, temporal reality can only be transformed to the extent that it comes to inhabit the present field (Civitarese, 2008).

If at a certain point, a classmate by whom the patient feels bullied has to enter the session, I could only consider it (as long as an analysis, or rather the state of the setting, has meaning) as a functioning taken on in a place in the field and enacted by the patient himself as a potentially disturbing identity, or by me as a disturbing presence for him.

If an experienced analyst finds himself cutting short a session with a relatively mute patient, I can only think in terms of a silent abuse which the analyst is suffering and therefore trying to withdraw the abused container (himself) from the abusive content. A sort of extreme "Maria Goretti" defence.

If a patient were to tell me he is going to build something by gathering up and organising all the bricks scattered on the terrace, I would visualise the bricks as the mad parts[3] which the patient is trying to organise and make useable for a project.

Staying on row C always allows the possibility of "dreaming", "visualising other possibilities with the mind's eye or the alpha function."

If an inhibited and hyper-controlling patient tells me about a "button" that's about to come off, I will certainly think of the big emotional bang[4] that he's scared of, and I would let myself be guided by these semantic-olfactory trails which all speech and every story are full of.

I remember a drawing by a girl of the trunk and crown of a tree which suddenly looked like a volcano erupting lava, and which after two years of therapy suggested a landscape viewed through an open window, from where a large number of small trees could be seen with their own crowns-of-lava: the proto-emotional main volcano had been broken down into many containable little volcanoes, as if it had been possible to "de-storm" the hurricane of beta elements and to transform it into discrete, containable components which could be thought about in terms of different, depictable emotions.

The auspicious dream: or the dream edging towards the Bunga-bunga girls

Marina is a brilliant patient but has areas of inhibition (behind which lumps of incontinence can be glimpsed).

An image which comes to me at the end of the session is a photograph by Doisneau in which a line of bare-chested girls is standing in front of an impresario who will or will not take them on depending on their beauty.

The next day Marina tells me she's had a dream: she was the country house of very wealthy friends and realised that, in order to escape from a gang of dangerous individuals, she had to give them an "inlaid Madonna", and then she saw a girl near a cube, uncertain whether or not to climb up on it.

Here my intervention was immediate: she seems to be opting to hand over the Madonna in exchange for the cubist!

In fact, the cubist remains to be discovered with at least a micro-camouflage.

The dream and the stone egg

The patient tells me a dream in which she is in a landscape like that of *The Shining*, with snow all around, and she has to be taken by taxi right up to the gate of a villa. She's a bit scared. There are constructions all around her with transvestites and prostitutes inside. She is afraid that the taxi-driver won't accompany to the gate, afraid of the cold and the atmosphere of suspense.

I comment, "It seems to you that, from a certain point of view, analysis could feel like a cold, disturbing place where you don't know what to expect, only clumps of excitation, but the frozen landscape isn't being transformed into Mediterranean *maquis*."

She replies, "I'm thinking about the advert for Smart cars where they showed a sequence of clips where someone's trying to kill the driver from the back seat and then a voice says, 'It's better when there's nobody behind you!' It's like an anti-advert for analysis."

"Then," she adds, "I'm thinking of a film with Laura Morante, maybe *The Refuge* or something like that, where a young woman went to a house where she discovered that terrible things had happened, and in the ventilation shafts lived a horrible girl, a monster, who stole other people's food and ate it. At first, the very rational heroine didn't believe it, but then she had to accept that the house was inhabited by this terrible ghost that's old now. Then I remember Jack Nicholson in *The Shining* writing the same phrase thousands of times over: 'The morning has gold in its mouth.' That's how his wife knew he was mad."

"So then," I add, "analysis isn't only the cold, disturbing place but also the place where a madman repeats the same things over and over and where there are terrifying ghosts."

"But really," she goes on, "I feel fine here with you. And besides you're legendary for always keeping the temperature at maximum."

"Well," I add, "I was thinking that in the town where I was born, there was a cinema, the Emerald, with two screens. If you were in cinema A you heard the sounds coming from cinema B, and sometimes you'd be watching a Bergman film and yells from a film about Geronimo would be coming from 'next door' or screams from a film like *The Shining*, or *Psycho*. I think we need to become experts in cinema B, the only one that really interests us."

"And in the film I was telling you about," she adds, "there was also a marble egg that fell down and left a mark on a wooden step on the staircase, and it was a sign that what had happened was 'true'."

To which I add, "It's true that other terrible things happen in cinema B, the eggs are made of stone or marble, and there's no way to fertilise them but, even so, that may be the cinema that's waiting for us."

Stefania's bald patches

Stefania suffers from baldness which causes her quite a few difficulties. Sometimes her hair grows normally, but at other times holes start to appear in it, growing larger until they merge with each other. One day she brings a dream in which she is looking down from a helicopter at a zoo with cages and animals that are so furry that you can't tell one species from another. After a time she decides to make another trip in the helicopter, and notices that there are other parts of the zoo with no cages, and the animals that should have been in them "seem to have been sucked back into the earth".

I have created two maps of the situations described by Stefania (Figures 9.1 and 9.2).

Naturally the graphical reconstructions are mine, but I think they are a good explanation of what the patient wanted to express: every so often her emotions are eradicated and interred, and in their place, there's a void, the patch with no fur.

From time to time the tiger, the lion, and the gazelle (each of these species standing for an emotion) will lose their fur. Every time an emotion is buried it seems that the map on the furry hide reproduces the phenomenon exactly.

Marilena's inhibited femininity

I would like to describe the operations which succeed in liberating a patient from the syndrome of absent femininity.

Marilena tells me that she has been given a fine, which she is pleased about because she is proud of having transgressed, instead of always being considered a good girl, studious and reliable.

What a disappointment when it turns out that the fine was for her brother, who had borrowed her car! She feels like a "potato". I tell her that maybe she is tired of seeing herself, or being seen by others, as a potato and would like to de-potato herself.

"How do you do that?"

"If a potato wanted to be a nobler, more sought-after tuber, what would it aspire to be?"

"A truffle," answers Marilena straightaway.

The potato is always there, available, easy to find, doesn't cost much. But the truffle is rare and you have to search for it, it smells really good, but it's not always available, you have to want it, search for it, and it costs!

And so Marilena starts to be de-potatoed, and one day finds herself giving slightly seductive answers to her boss in the insurance company where she works,

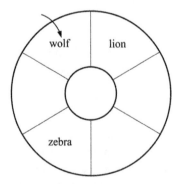

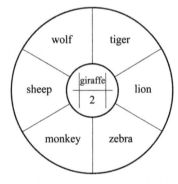

FIGURE 9.1 The zoo as it appears in the first part of the dream

FIGURE 9.2 The zoo as it appears in the second part of the dream

and he immediately notices how loosened up and sparkling she has become.

It is at this point – to introduce a more overt way of talking – that I dare to mention the fact that her femininity seems to be less afraid of getting fined, and that it seems to be daring to express itself, and I add, "So maybe your underwear should stop being the kind your granny would buy but, thinking along French lines, you should use *Agent Provocateur*."

"That's what I did last week when I was at a convention in Nice. Not only that, but the truffle makes me think that I've had enough of my granny's cologne. I need to start looking for a perfume of my own, like in the Brad Pitt ads for Chanel No. 5, even if it is a bit old-fashioned."

Depression

I'd like to go back to the theme of depression that I addressed earlier. You often need to work backwards to find the underground lake of depression, and we need to proceed downwards from the defences. We have a whole series of anti-depressive mechanisms, to name only the main ones.

- Sexoril
- Eateraril
- Excitoril
- Drugatil
- Sadomasochil
- Alcolil

Each of these therapies, self-prescribed and self-administered, is capable of keeping the depression-monster at bay for a certain length of time.

We have an infinite quantity of literary and cinematic works on the subject and I could hardly not start with Heinrich Mann's *Professor Unrat* and its unforgettable film version (von Sternberg's *The Blue Angel*).

Stefano is on orthopaedic surgeon aged 38, brilliant in his field, who for some years has been in a relationship with a physiotherapeutic physician in the department where he works. The physician, Lorena, lives with a very hot-tempered physiotherapist. The relationship with Lorena is described as bringing him to states of ecstasy (she is the most beautiful woman in the world) and then plunging him into furious despair (she's a slut, she's going to leave me). The relationship is a continuous collision and – with the full collaboration of both – strongly sadomasochistic and excitatory, which allows them to lap at the lake of depression without diving into it, by means of this to-and-fro of torment and ecstasy on an emotional rollercoaster.

He had been depressed and apathetic as a child, with marked obsessive and ritualistic traits with which he "contained" or, it would be truer to say, exorcised a violent anger towards his father who had left to live with another woman. This "anger" had never been dealt with, not least because it was woven into the atmosphere he breathed in the family, where the father's desertion was continually condemned. But the same anger was in turn a vital reaction to the intolerable experiences of abandonment, pain, and despair which were the unspoken element in the air he had breathed.

When he was little he had gone through a period of real depression (the breakdown that had already happened, as Winnicott would say), which he had emerged from by the use of excitatory modalities

But why is the depressive lake not often crossed? What are its waters made of? I think they are made out of a mixture of anger-resentment-despair-pain which cannot be worked through, as if it were believed that the process of mourning (the only one that could bring us to the other side of the lake) is impossible to manage or bear (Ferruta, 2014) because mourning and depression get blocked and collide with the mourning for death which cannot be worked through.

Perhaps health in this area would entail a transition from the "constant struggle" of youth to the "constant mourning" of adulthood, which would enable an appropriate digestion of that polymer of anger-resentment-despair-pain which forms the depressive monster's habitat.

A working-through/payment in instalments is the most we are able to do, accepting that small anaesthesias are sometimes helpful and (why not?) necessary.

Supervision and high water

A supervision begins with a colleague who, as if *en passant*, makes a comment on the present "high water" in Venice. Then she mentions a paper she is to give at a conference on "splitting and integration", and lastly talks about her patient.

The patient himself starts by saying that he has been deeply disturbed by the fact that one of his own patients has killed himself. He goes on to talk about another patient who needs antidepressants, and after a brief pause says he is again thinking about the possibility of a training analysis.

It seems obvious that the analyst I am supervising feels this is a difficult moment with her patient: it's high water, and there is a problem of splitting/ integration.

The patient is affected by a marked, desperate depression with which he is not in contact. He is only in contact with the antidepressant which, in this case, would be the "training analysis", although, in his own analysis, this could also have the meaning (the inflection) of teaching him how to overcome his depression.

Suicide or homicide

Tina begins the session by asking what the crumbs are that she's found on the couch and the floor. It needs the CID.

Then she talks about moments of black depression she has had, and finally says that a ten-year-old boy has tried to kill himself by jumping off the balcony. Then she talks about two depressed patients she saw last week.

The boy had a tumour that broke in the fall.

I tell her that it seems as if, in addition to the "Thursday syndrome" we are used to (on Thursdays she always ends up talking about abandonments, children alone, separations), we now have a clear "Monday syndrome" consisting of everything that had depressed her over the weekend, dark emotions which have proliferated inside her, suggesting thoughts of death and depression.

At this point she talks about the famous story of General Petraeus's betrayal and I can tell her that this is just what the start of the session was about: it needs the CIA or the CID to discover my Thursday or Monday betrayal that might lead her to do away with me or with herself.

Of course, that's how it is, and more loudly I say "What else?" [in English], imitating a famous advertisement.

Marco and his double

Marco works as a pastry chef, which he enjoys; but he soon shows a hidden side. The therapist notices the slovenly way he dresses, his irregular teeth and dilated pupils.

He had asked for therapy because of self-harming behaviour which he engages in every time his internal temperature starts to rise; as a result he has had several admissions to a trauma ward.

Gradually as the therapy proceeds, Marco tells the story of his earlier life in which he had kept the worst kind of company, people with whom had often risked going to prison. He had been both a drug-user and dealer.

Now he is in a relationship with Tiziana who works in a gym. Their affair is extremely violent, full of jealousy, rage, and furious quarrels which seem to have the same excitatory function that cocaine used to have.

He has trouble recognising different emotions, which present themselves to him as a "proto-aggregate" and urge him to find a way of evacuating them, often in characteropathic, violent, criminal acts.

He gradually seems to start recognising how much he is in the grip of jealousy, anger, and the experience of exclusion, and he engages in a real rodeo with these emotions as he tries not to be unseated by his actions.

The antidepressant function of these excitations becomes ever clearer, until he has a dream which sees him furiously pumping up tyres that are lying on the ground. The harder he pumps the more they deflate, and so he increases the force and speed of his pumping, until he realises that the first thing he needs to do is find the hole in each tyre.

This hole is later revealed as the lack of someone who would turn up promptly whenever he was in pain and despair. For some time, before he started to work through this experience, Marco resorted to self-tortures which he inflicted on himself with the most diverse feelings of guilt: he beat himself up so as not to feel the pain, covering it up by self-harm.

Working through this sense of emptiness and loneliness, Marco starts to take account of his own furious anger, which finds a regulator in the "traffic light dream": the Hulk finds that he has suddenly turned red because he's reflecting a red light that's telling him to stop. He steadily becomes able to distinguish and contain his various emotions and can "fantasise" instead of acting. These fantasies go from "being ready to stab the new girlfriend he loves and about whom he is terribly jealous" to erotomanic and perverse fantasies which act as therapy for the underlying situation of deficit-depression.

This is what it will be possible to work through by means of a series of dreams which will put emotions and images in place of mute and criminal actions.

Mario and the fires

Mario telephones me while he is still in hospital, where he was admitted because, during a firework display while on holiday in Nice with his family, he was hit full in the chest by a rocket. His chest had been badly lacerated, together with second- and third-degree burns, and his wife had also been very badly burned.

He tells me they are both on the way to recovery but that he is calling me because he would like to know if his three young daughters, who were present at the accident, have been traumatised.

I offer him and his wife an appointment and they tell me the details of the accident, caused by a rocket which flew too low and hit them on the balcony from where they should have been able to enjoy the show.

I try to learn more about the three daughters who are not showing any particular signs of post-traumatic distress.

Moving into "free conversation" ("talking as dreaming" as Ogden would say) I learn that about ten years ago, Mario had had another accident: he had been run over by a lorry in a layby on the motorway. In both cases, he describes the enormous force of the impact of the rocket and the lorry. On that earlier occasion he had likewise ended up in intensive care, between life and death. Then he had recovered. Carrying on with the free-wheeling conversation, they tell me they have always, over twenty years of marriage, had furious quarrels, real hurricanes... How could they not, he being from Palermo and she from Tunisia? Two passionate characters, and violent in their passions, I would say.

At this point the conversation takes on a different Gestalt: what are the implications of their emotional voltage – two hundred thousand volts, which sometimes gets them hospitalised with its burns – for the way their life develops?

How traumatic and potentially dangerous are these emotional storms which crash over them? An oneiric listening allows a totally different view.

Marta and the "sender of messages"

Marta arrives, asking for therapy because she is in the grip of "a delusion": a "sender of messages" is in love with her and is going to marry her.

As time passes, it seems that the "sender of messages" goes into action whenever there is something in the communication or in factual reality that Marta does not understand, and she uses him to get out of a confusing and disorienting situation.

Rather than a delusion or hallucination, over time the "sender of messages" becomes something ("an auxiliary SIM card that takes over" when the main SIM card gets disconnected) or someone who supplies understanding in order to stop her going wrong when there are too many possible directions to choose from.

During the therapy, the "sender of messages" sometimes becomes the therapist, in whom there is much emotional investment, and at other times a "supplementary function" which keeps her safe from a psychic breakdown.

After a long therapeutic process, she brings her first dream in which a six-year-old girl (the age of the therapy), feared to be seriously ill, was found to have many healthy features and had been placed in a class with healthy children.

At the same time, her sister Tina starts coming into the sessions. Marta trusts her, confides in her, and is helped by her, and her voice (the voice of the therapist) seems increasingly to replace that of the "sender of messages".

Then she says that for some time her friends have been using the diminutive of her name, Martina, which seems to be a prelude to integration with her own healthier functions (her sister Tina).

At this point, to her family's surprise, the patient resumes her interrupted university studies and gets a degree.

The therapy continues with a Martina who goes on broadening her own existential horizons.

On the nephrology ward

Luca is a 27-year-old nurse who asks for therapy because he has unexpectedly and contemptuously been left by his Icelandic girlfriend Reny.

Already being inclined to believe that people thought little of him and that he wasn't worth much, he was planning to prescribe himself a course of anti-depressants and asking for leave to go to Afghanistan.

But the depressive breakdown which intervenes stops him doing anything: he lies in bed crying and saying he can't live without Reny.

From the start, the communication is perceived as his being unable to live without kidneys,[5] without those purgative-metabolic functions which his very beautiful and energetic girlfriend had performed for him for a long time. The therapy becomes a sort of dialysis for him, enabling him to metabolise – and before that, to filter out – and identify the toxic substances which were in danger of building up and putting him into a "depressive coma"; in this way, he can acknowledge his inability to live alone, to bear being abandoned.

After several months of therapy he gets engaged to a beautiful girl from Barcelona who works in the same place. It is only at this point – after the emergency dialysis – that he will ask for a kidney transplant, in the sense that he decides to address his problems more determinedly by asking to have an analysis.

The dilapidated bell-tower

A patient aged about 35 tells me in irritation that her mother has said to her, "You've reached the age where you can't keep putting off the important decisions about your life…"

In the next session she tells me she didn't know why she was feeling irritated and her boyfriend was even more so.

There is a silence, after which I say, "Do you want me to tell you the dream your boyfriend had last night?"

"What do you mean?!" She has a rush of paranoia. "Were you listening to our conversation at the bar when we were having breakfast!? How do you know my boyfriend had a dream and told me about it?"

"Well, do you want to hear it or not?"

"Of course I do," she replies.

This is the dream: a dilapidated bell-tower like one on a church is being rebuilt, and a clock is being hung on it in the usual place, but at first it has no hands (like in *Wild Strawberries*). Then the hands are added and show midday. (This is all the product of a piece of visual imagination which came to me right at the start of the session.)

The patient is astonished. "No! I don't believe it!"

Enzo said he dreamed about "a dilapidated church, one of those old ones with a bell-tower that was being rebuilt, and you were waiting for me there."

I reply, "It's usually the groom who waits for the bride, but that's all right too."

This unconscious and half-serious "oneiric dance" led us back to the theme of her mother, the theme of time, the theme of mourning for time.

Then the patient says it seems important to her that the clock was showing 12 and not 7 or 9, or even 17 or 20: there was time to do things.

(The implication is obviously that this refers to her taking responsibility.)

Marriage, children, existential decisions, the biological clock, time to mourn the loss of omnipotence. The Church in our culture with its reminders of time: baptism/marriage/funeral, etc.

The split-off part of Ale(ssandra)

A patient, Ale, is brought up in supervision: she has had quite serious anorexia. She says that when she was in a hospital unit she had ended up in a room with a boy who had had a pantoclastic episode.

The anorexia had later reduced somewhat.

Then a boy came into her life who smoked joints and drank.

What then emerges is a long history of violence in the family and the grandparents' family, also caused by alcoholism and depression.

The picture which immediately presents itself to me is the following: beside Ale there is a part/function σ which has been split off (-ssandro) and is not easy for Ale to contain or digest.

So, all that is left for Ale is to describe (for those who have ears to listen) this function (the boy with the destructive episode in her hospital room) and then to describe the violence of "ssandro" whom she tries to manage with various defence mechanisms: starvation, drinking, smoking joints; in other words, anorexia, alcoholism, manic behaviour.

The real violence and abuse are, fundamentally, what Ale has received and continues to receive from "ssandro", and the aim of the analysis will be the development of those tools which will permit "ssandro" to be contained and metabolised.

Notes

1 A blood-drenched Mafia novel by Giuseppe Ferrandino, published in 1993 under the pseudonym Nicola Calata.
2 Translator's note: the play on *catafalco* and *falco* is naturally closer in Italian.
3 Translator's note: here the play is on *mattoni* (bricks) and *matto* (mad).
4 Translator's note: here *bottone* (button) suggests *botto* (bang).
5 Translator's note: kidneys are *reni* in Italian.

10

RANDOM THOUGHTS ON TECHNIQUE AND OTHER MATTERS

This chapter does not contain innovative ideas but aims to try and enable the reader to encounter the miracle we find in Calvino's book *If on a Winter's Night a Traveller*: that is, a powerful recreation of what happens in the construction of the analytic field, where many readers contribute to the reading of many different chapters. In other words, I would like to highlight the missing parts of the chapter and its paragraphs so that everyone can fill them in with their own thoughts, questions, doubts as they occur while reading: or so that we can take a step forward from what was read in the previous chapter. For example, is there any sense in the distinction between easy and difficult dreams? Or could this be a trap? And so on, in the hope that, once the chapter has been read, both the way of perceiving the text and the reader himself may have changed.

Contents and modalities: what film are we going to see?

Luca is a patient in the fifth year of psychotherapy with an effective colleague who comes to see me at a moment of difficulty he is unable to get through.

He tells me that good work has been done with Luca, steadily freeing him from a vengeful-symbiotic nucleus which had been undermining his developmental potential for a long time.

Working through these features had led him to make satisfying progress in therapy, both in his mental functioning and in his professional and emotional life. A date had been agreed for the end of the therapy a year in advance, to the mutual satisfaction of patient and analyst; but on his return from the summer holiday, not only had Luca plunged back into his original symptomatology, but he had started to oscillate between a violent erotic excitation and an open violence in his previously affectionate relationships.

Pornographic fantasies and acts follow on from one another, sexually perverse fantasies and acts invade the sessions which become scenes of violent, bloody disputes.

The analyst is invaded in a persecutory fashion and works on these contents, aware that the initial symptoms can reappear in the concluding phase, but this is frankly too much, and he is worried and distressed on the patient's behalf. In the midst of this uproar, he loses the patient's key communication: "It's sad to lose someone." And, in fact, he does not understand that the patient keeps taking him to see pornographic or violent "films" (narrative derivatives) as an excitatory alternative to mourning his loss, the end of the therapy which he is unable to come to terms with.

It is only after realising the *way* in which the patient is avoiding pain, the way in which he is taking the therapist to see "films" full of sex/eroticism/pornography or else of violence, that he can bring the patient up close to his painful experiences of loss, nostalgia, lack (Civitarese, 2011).

Only at this point will the patient replace the orgiastic contents ("he deflowers her from in front and from behind … a woman – in a dream – slips a finger up my backside … and offers me her breast … two pleasures … etc.) with contents which begin to speak about possibly getting close to the mourning for loss and the end of therapy ("I'm reading a strange French book, *Morts imaginaires* by Schneider, which tells about the last moments of 36 writers based on their lives and works").

And so, once the "narrative genre" changes, so does the way of approaching mourning and loss, as will be highlighted some weeks later, when he goes to a multiplex and hesitates over whether to see a very violent porn film or *Amour*, starring Jean-Louis Trintignant, about the illness and death of an old couple who have been together for many years.

What has been described here is of interest because it reminds us that it is not only the *content* of the narrative which concerns us, but also the *narrative mode*. This is true in all cases. If a patient keeps telling us about *The Miracle of Marcellino*, [1] or the many variations on the way this fable could be narrated, we should pay attention to this narrative choice and reflect on the other narrative scenarios that are being obscured by this choice. If we attend only to the content we run the risk of never leaving the "fable" of the ill-treated child which is so fundamental but may rule out other possible literary/narrative/visual-cinematic genres.

This is not unlike the problem of the necessary oscillation between *contents* and *modes* in those patients who present with a base fantasy which they reiterate in every possible version.

Thinking about Lory, a patient of Domenico Chianese the fable is constantly that of someone always being excluded by someone else who is busy (or likes to be busy) with other thoughts, leaving Lory perennially bathed in jealousy, exclusion, and rage (Chianese, 1997).

It is obvious that this Gestalt must be worked through without getting tiresomely bound up in all its various narrative permutations, but at a certain point it will be just as essential to encourage access to other modes and other "possible worlds" which are nevertheless there in a potential state and, Bion would say, waiting for a thinker.

The hieroglyphic mother and the Rosetta Stone

Carla is a seven-year-old girl who was identified when she started school as having globally delayed language development, including a difficulty in reading and memorising vowels and certain consonants.

She has a younger sister who suffers from moments of intense fear.

The mother is described as warm and affectionate, alternating with moments of incontinence.

Immediately the idea takes shape of a child with difficulty in reading the state of mind of a mother who was sometimes (U) welcoming and receptive, and sometimes (∩), frankly convex, repelling, rejecting.

The mother herself also seems unable to orient herself in relation to Carla's state of mind, describing her as a puzzling child.

For Carla, the affective foundation seems disorienting, with an alternation between unpredictable emotional states UUNUNN UUNUNNNCCUCC which have not allowed her a secure support for understanding the variations she encounters: how is Mummy at this moment? What can I expect from her? And also the symmetrical question: what are my feelings towards Mummy? Do I hate her or can't I do without her? The basic "insole" and its shape are fundamental for developing the ability to distinguish between one's own and other people's emotions.

The indecipherable mother is an impossible hieroglyph to read in her alternation between concave and convex, partially concave, partially convex. She exposes the child to a situation like that of someone going home by car and driving up to the garage without knowing whether to expect the door to be open or whether it's a *trompe-l'oeil* that the car is going to crash into: will it be the hypothetical sequence UUNCNNCUN or the actual underlying level hypothetical sequence ♀♂♀♀♀♀♂♂?

This narrative of serious difficulty in reading the mind of the other is further presented in a double story previously told by the mother, in great distress, as follows: Carla's teacher has reported that Carla seems unable to distinguish her classmates, even though she has a reasonably good relationship with them. She goes up to them calling them "Friend" in an undifferentiated way. There is no clear recognition of Filippo, Luigi, or Marcello, just as there is none of the vowels or of the letters b or d, which she always gets the wrong way round.

Carla's father confirms this "reading", remembering a journey he'd made to Australia where he met many different people in friend's houses, but formal introductions were never made and instead people addressed everyone else as "Mate", resulting in a certain degree of undifferentiation.

I should also mention the fear felt by part of her (the little sister) when she finds herself in indecipherable situations. In the consulting room, is she with a "friend" or a Bluebeard? What does her grandfather mean when he says "I'll give you a party"?[2]

It is also true that her parents, while deficient in the function of distinguishing and recognising states of mind, have been sufficiently capable of transforming the swarms of sensoriality without having to start compulsively reading the details, as happens in the paranoid situation.

The situations described here quickly start to occur in the session, where Carla doesn't know whether she wants to hug or throttle the therapist, who is himself unable to work out what the girl is going to do next. It is true that the session will gradually become the place for discrimination, where Carla and the therapist will learn to understand, grasp, and differentiate the components of the basic emotional grammar which is developing as the session's affective text.

At one point, Carla goes through a brief para-delusional period in which she fears that people (and emotions) are camouflaged, and some characters from a television serial start to appear, a gang of kidnappers called "the wolf", "the pig", etc., but Carla wants to camouflage them.

At the same time, she starts playing games in which she puts fierce animals (which she can now distinguish from domesticated ones) inside toy saucepans, as if she felt the need to cook them, or as Bion would say, the need to tame wild thoughts.

The field

The field is also the place for all the potential identities of patient and analyst, but this does not mean that all potential identities must come to life or be integrated: sometimes it is appropriate for them to stay split off, cut off in the field itself for as long as this is helpful to the development of mental life (Ferro, et al., 2007; 2011; 2013).

In order for a narrative to develop, there are many possible stories which must be "narcotised" so that the prevailing story and "child" of the two co-narrators can come to life and develop.

I have spoken on other occasions about how there are two "*loci*" of mental creativity in a Bionian metapsychology: the place where beta elements, the carriers of all the sensoriality, are transformed by alpha function into pictograms (subunits of dream-thought in the waking state) and the place where the narrative derivative in all its infinite variety – depending on the length of its leash – moves away from or stays close to waking dream-thought within the field (Bezoari and Ferro, 1997; Corrao, 1998; Di Chiara, 2003).

The psychoanalytic church: or fear

The characteristic of repetition, often empty repetition, and the characteristic of celebrating the known are legitimate defences: faced with the innovations of an Ogden (who only received the Sigourney prize in 2012) there is nothing for it but to question one's own knowledge, one's own theory of technique, and one's technique itself – which would be highly painful and laborious. Otherwise we attack the new "genius" in every possible way for daring to disturb our pre-constituted and established set-up.

The second mode, the one that leads to the dismissal of the not-known ("This isn't psychoanalysis") enormously slows down the development and expansion of psycho-analysis in the direction of new pathologies. The former solution is calming, keeping us anchored to the known, but preventing new developments (Bolognini, 2002a).

Periodically a new caesura is recognised, but with incredible slowness. Even the "relational turn" in psychoanalysis has not yet become a shared patrimony for the priestly caste of "real psychoanalysis", given their unconscious (emotional) interests. Nothing from Galileo onwards for the development of science.

The ability to discriminate

A woman patient with all the advantages – intellectual, physical, and professional – has not been able to have a satisfactory relationship with a man. Now she hides her own attractiveness, the gifts at her disposal, even her profession (solicitor), because she is afraid that other people may exploit her: in fact, she lives a life reduced to a minimum.

What she seems afraid of is others' envy, but what seems even more to be the problem is made clear in a dream where her friends have lost their sense of smell.

This is the problem: she has no nose for people! She cannot intuit who she is dealing with, which leads her to make crazy blunders and always end up with the wrong man. It is only at this point that she recalls a habitual "practice" in her family when they still lived in Sicily: the children were told that grownups could tell whether or not they were telling the truth by smelling their heads. It seems to be the lack of exactly this discriminatory ability ("having a nose!") which has stopped her "discriminating", intuiting, catching *en passant* the characteristics of the person to whom she is relating. This olfactory sense has been "done away with" out of a need not to detect the false nature of her parents' relationship (each of whom had a number of lovers) and the false relationship she had with them, which is later revealed by a dream set in Dubai, where it's not possible to tell what is real and what is fake, followed by another dream set in an exhibition of "plastics" where again there's no distinction between what is real and what is fake.

It is precisely this lack of a nose which has made her embark on affairs with men who have turned out in the end to be skilful con artists. At this point she has a dream in which some stem cells are transplanted into her nose, physically devel-oping it into something like Cyrano de Bergerac's nose, but also turning into olfactory cells which enable her to recognise what other people have in their heads: truth or lies.

Un-disguising

The session begins with a story about how in the middle of the night Lara was woken by her dog which had heard a male dog climbing the stairs.

Then Lara remembers a dream in which some secret agents wanted to come into her house and she decided not to resist. One moment they were at the door, the next they were inside.

I ask her if she has felt that in previous sessions I've been putting her under too much pressure to talk about subjects she has tended to avoid. We have spoken in the past about a male colleague with the surname Di Femmina, and then moved on to the perfume Femina. She denies that this alarmed her and veers off, though still on the subject of femininity, to talk about how Penelope Cruz had been able to disguise herself as an Italian character in the film based on the novel *Don't Move*, [3] and made herself look really ugly. Lara, who has shares in a multinational pharmaceutical company, goes on to talk about the new low-dose Cialis just released by Lilly.

At this point I can't resist the invitation to make an active and penetrating interpretation, and I tell her that to me she seems very like Penelope Cruz, but that she does all she can to disguise herself and is now starting to un-disguise herself. However, it's true that this creates problems: Penelope Cruz avoids certain risks by going incognito or disguised as an Italian.

"But I'd like a man like Guido in *One day at a time* [4] who's able to love without being frightening," says Lara.

"Whereas men," I observe, "the most bulldozing ones, cause alarm by just going upstairs, even when you seem to have decided not to resist. Besides," I add, "it doesn't mean that men have to, or want to, make a D-Day landing in Normandy."

She concludes by saying, "I'll try to un-disguise myself."

Here she seems to have adopted the disguising of Penelope Cruz and femininity so as not to fall victim to the Moroccans in *La Ciociara*:[5] in other words, violent emotions which she fears will abuse her, and she thinks that disguising the container will guarantee its safety. The -F seems to be a way of saying to the *Landsknechte*, [6] "There are no 'obscure objects of desire' here."

In the next session, Lara brings a dream in which she is in a room with the windows bricked up and no way out. I say that perhaps I had pressed her too hard the day before with our talk about un-disguising. (In this session she looks particularly elegant and feminine.)

She goes on to talk about some colleagues at the multinational company who like being with her but only talk about work, whereas she would like them to become friends she could meet and talk freely to, without any set objective in mind. I understand this as the patient's desire for less pressure and to be able to "talk as friends". And so I let myself go in the conversational flow, only realising afterwards that this is exactly what Ogden means by *talking as dreaming*. The conversation runs from McEwan to Mazzantini, from scientific articles of varying importance to Bollas (writing as a novelist rather than as a psychoanalyst) and his book *Dark at the End of the Tunnel* which tells the story of a terrorist who suffers from panic attacks which keep stopping him from setting up the explosions he has planned. The main character, who is an analyst, does not know which is best: leave the patient with his inhibitory symptom or "cure" him, at the cost of enabling him to commit his murders? In turn, I tell the story of a German analyst learning in a session with a Baader-Meinhof activist that the patient was planning a bombing attack the next day, and lying awake all night not knowing what to do: warn the police or respect patient confidentiality? Despite being sleepless all night, the analyst did not warn the forces of law and order. The next day at 15.15 (and only at that moment do I realise that 15.15 is the time of my own patient's appointments) the patient knocks on the door and says, "I didn't plant the bomb. There was no explosion. I didn't hear my alarm, so I overslept."

Only at this point do I realise the relevance of our talking as dreaming and am able to say, "But are we sure that the explosion of your femininity would have all that many victims?"

Traumas

In the example of the "firework" trauma, O is the emotional turbulence which is unrepresentable despite having had an initial concrete and factual narrative. Subsequently, it had been transformed by the analyst's dreaming ear into a dream which, from a certain point of view, was a lie in relation to the unknowable that lay upstream.

The whirlwind of beta elements could be O and, later on, could be attempts to alphabetise the unknowable. I repeat: the beta-whirlwind is transformed, passing through Column 2, perhaps by way of Row 3, and perhaps pausing in square 2/3. This whole process is fostered by immersion in an unsaturated climate-atmosphere of negative capability of the analyst's listening.

The same story is true for any traumatic reality, which must pass through Column 2, Row 3, and their intersection in order to be transformed and rendered thinkable instead of obscuring. This would also be true of Lara's situation and her ♀ as defence of an O which she fears would be explosive.

Ambivalence

The moment came when I needed to tell Laura about the Christmas holidays.

Then, when she knows the dates, she tells me the previous night's dream. She was in an aeroplane, going on holiday, and then found herself on an island. On one side there were the passengers' baggage trolleys and a girl was complaining about how little she was being allowed to take with her. She showed what she had in her trolley and in a handbag: a comb, brush, sticking plasters and other little things she said would have to be enough to get her through two weeks of holiday.

Then she goes on to tell me about having acted (as a lawyer) on behalf of a girl who had been abused and thrown out of the house by her father, and had decided to lodge a formal complaint against him at 15.30 (the time of Laura's session). Both the emotional series are true: on the one hand she feels ready and equipped to spend two weeks in isolation, but it is equally true that she is feel expelled and abused because of the holidays she must put up with. But it is now possible to talk with Laura about these emotions and join them up since they have all the rights of citizens.

Biological markers of time and connected defences

Once upon a time the "ages of man" were marked like the seasons, each season having its own characteristics, its own fruits. Now, with the advent of medicine and surgery, this has all vanished. For women, the end of menstruation used to be an inescapable marker, but now it can be almost indefinitely postponed by hormone replacement therapy. Men had to resign themselves to erectile dysfunctions as hailing the third age, but now with drugs like Viagra they can have erections almost *sine die*. Hair loss, precarious teeth, sagging bellies and breasts – to cite only the most obvious features – can easily be put right with plastic surgery.

The denial of time's passing and of life's relative transience are very strong defences against something telling us (or trying to tell us) that the last stops, the final season, are on their way. White-haired old men lose their heads over women who conceal their own age under make-up: it's all part of the seductive game which has no other goal than the illusion that autumn and winter can be deferred. Mourning, grief, and loss are disguised; everything ends up as a crazy merry-go-round of endless manic excitation.

But deep down everyone knows, or should know, that this trick can't go on forever, and that brute reality has to return. A strategy of small griefs is replaced by a strategy of postponed mourning, sometimes to an extreme degree.

Sabrina and the telephone

I am unexpectedly forced to cancel Sabrina's last two sessions of the week, and unable to give her any advance notice of this.

"Oh, no problem, I know we'll meet on Monday," is Sabrina's initial comment.

The next thing she tells me is about mothers suffering from postnatal depression and their various outcomes, from suicide to full recovery. Then she talks about a book by Stern which points out the risks involved in babies being separated from their mothers. Next, she tells me about a time when her father spent a year away from home because of work and how, as a little girl, she was afraid that bad people would chop him into pieces. And lastly, she tells me that when she was a child she witnessed a furious argument when her father had gone on week's holiday by himself and her mother had been seized with furious jealousy, thinking there must have been another woman involved. In any case, it had been a kind of betrayal.

I think it may be appropriate to make an interpretative intervention, though lightly, and pick up all these themes in connection with my cancellation of the sessions. Instead of denying or being disturbed by my intervention, the patient responds by telling me how happy she had been when her father came back from one of his absences and gave her a toy telephone on wheels. It seems that for Sabrina communication brings relief, unlike what happens with other patients who are less open to communication.

A digression about dreaming

As is well known, it is central to Freud's *Remembering, Repeating and Working Through* (1914b) and to his later elaborations, that what cannot be remembered will be repeated. In the end, it is this key concept which enables very early experiences (which by their nature cannot be remembered) to gain access to the consulting room by means of the transference. His conceptualisations about declarative and implicit memory are also well known.

The first session has barely started when Mirella, who traumatically lost her mother, insists that I accept payment in advance for the first year of analysis!

The centrality of the dream in analysis has always concerned the dream already dreamed which, whatever its various shades, has always been considered a valuable source of information revealing the events of the past.

The dream in analysis has always been seen as a dream dreamed by the patient and, at most, as a countertransference dream by the analyst (Barale and Ferro, 1992).

At a certain point the valuable concept of enactment arrived, in which some-thing which cannot be remembered is re-actualised jointly by the analytic couple, enabling both the re-appropriation of something which had remained outside thinkability and its resolution, which then – passing from the here and now – allows us to go back to the scene which had been lost.

Without in the least denying the value of these tools which we all use, I would like to add a different perspective, as a subject for research: which is, the value of the dream that must be dreamed in the session by analyst and patient, a dream aimed at the future.

This dream is the true transformative event and it is hard to do, for several rea-sons: it puts into play the couple's creativity, but also all the obstacles to this crea-tivity, as well as casting doubt on the certainties and the supposedly scientific nature of analytic work.

Furthermore, this is precisely what Bion says both in his *Tavistock Seminars* and in the wonderful seminar held in Paris (1978).

When patients arrive with their realistic stories, it is our job (with them) to turn these into a dream. This journey towards oneiricisation is the continuous work of alphabetisation performed by the alpha function (or rather, by the alpha functions of the field) on the quanta of sensoriality brought by the patient and the analyst, although co-generated in the field.

I have described elsewhere all the operations linked to this work (Ferro, et al., 2013): the importance of reverie, the construction of dream-thought in the waking state (the sequence of oneiric pictograms), that sort of primary part-digestion that is done by the two minds' ruminating function. Ideally, all this should provide material that is already more metabolised so as to initiate the operations of trans-formation into dream in the session.

From this viewpoint, the patient's dream would only offer previously alphabe-tised material for the work of the dream in the session. What the patient recounts, what he or she acts, micro-acts, evacuates, and dreams are all pre-ingredients for the activation of the dream in the session.

Why is it so difficult for this concept to be shared? I think some of the answer lies in the strength of the earlier models, brilliantly displayed in cinematic form by Pabst in *Secrets of a Soul* and by Hitchcock in *Spellbound*. Moreover, reality is something which makes us feel safe: trauma, historical reconstruction, remembering real facts which explain us and permit insight.

Do you remember those socialist-realist paintings? In the end they offer security. We don't all love Chagall or Picasso, even though their reality is much truer than usual reality because it is made emotional: that is, passed through a gaze which does not deform but sees further!

Reality, facts, and memories have nothing to do with what has happened: which is something we'll never know! We will, however, be able to make a film of what is happening and of what could have happened. We are terrified of the idea that we are more like artists than scientists because science seems to provide a more dependable *ubi consistam*. Creativity, the provisional, transience terrify us, and art is always ahead of science in this.

Easy dreams

The sale of couches

A patient at the end of analysis has the following dream: she was in America, feeling good, and was happy with her boyfriend. Then she met another patient, a typical psychiatric case, who had a sticking plaster on her. The health services could no longer take care of this other patient, so my patient decided to look after her herself. Then there was a kind of auction where couches and armchairs were being sold – of no interest to her, but other people seemed to find it interesting. Then she went back to taking care of the other patient's wound.

It seems obvious that the patient now feels able to take care of her suffering parts, now that she is in the new world which analysis has allowed her to reach. Time is up for analysis, and the "couch and armchair" will be of interest to the other possible patients to whom she is gladly bequeathing her place.

The fracture: the undreamed dream

At the start of the first session after the holidays, a patient phones her analyst to say she has suffered a fracture in the mountains and will take a month to recover. She finds getting out of bed intolerably painful. The analyst can only accept this manifest script, but it is hard for her not to think that the summer holidays have been a fracture from which the patient has not found it easy to recover, and that getting up from the couch has been a very painful operation.

The bacteria and the polluted session

A patient starts a session by talking about how her dog has an infection in its front paws, caused – according to the vet – by an excess of bacteria which have colonised the micro-wounds in the paws.

Naturally, I have to choose between two possibilities: either to interpret the pollution of the setting (which was caused by some interpretative interventions of mine which had been too off-hand) or to come up with a more aseptic setting.

I choose the second option and at the end of the session the patient tells me that her dog is better, the therapy has worked and, apparently inadvertently, she says "thank you".

Difficult dreams

To attack or to communicate

For a long time, any infraction or breaking of the setting by the patient has been simplistically considered an "attack" on the setting itself. And this too is a way of avoiding the (not always easy) work of comprehension which other viewpoints might require from us.

For example, at the end of her analysis, before the final summer break, Lisa gives her analyst a cheque made out to herself.

It would be easy to place this in the category of "attack on the setting", but more complicated to try and find some more specific meanings: keeping the analyst in suspense and guaranteeing his return, but above all being able to express that she now feels able to fulfil the analyst's function herself, and ready to become her own analyst.

An analysis which communicates meanings and specific emotions is very different from a cafeteria-analysis which serves the same recipes to everyone.

This dream is followed by a dream I had that same night, and then by another dream of Lisa's.

The analyst's dream

I had a high-powered car which I had not allowed myself before. I got into it with a friend at my grandparents' house, perhaps by way of Tripoli.

I was pleased with this car (a Mercedes or perhaps a Maserati) and I met Glen Gabbard, with whom I exchanged some information, telling him about a "potential transference". Then I went back to my car. In both cases there is a new "power" I was able to draw on.

A psychotherapist and her patient

The morning after my dream Lisa keeps on talking about her daughter who has changed schools. Is this a good thing or not? Then she tells me that her sister (an experienced psychotherapist) is treating a girl with many problems who looks after every injured animal she comes across. The girl values her therapy greatly.

I am able to tell Lisa that yes, there's a girl in the dream with needs and sufferings, but also a psychotherapist able to take care of her. And perhaps her sister is actually herself, who has acquired the ability to take her own sufferings on board, and that it is time to change teachers and to make out the cheque to herself. She will be her own new therapist.

I can then link up this situation inside myself with my previous dream in which I likewise acknowledge a "strength" in me which I had not recognised before, one which enables me to adopt different viewpoints towards concepts which had previously been so true that I could never call them into question.

The transplant

Simona tells me about a very angry girl she has seen in hospital waiting for a lung transplant, so angry that the doctors are afraid she is capable of violence, even murder. I ask Simona if she feels like taking the lift with me down to the depths. Maybe we'll find a girl there, one for whom every Thursday brings the removal of a lung, and then she has to wait until Monday to have a new one transplanted into her.... On the ground floor there is only a distant vibration, but in the bowels of the earth it is lived with violent intensity.

Moreover, when a long is removed, how could you not have an outbreak of fury in which you want to kill everyone?

This evokes an associative cascade, from the fear she had lost her parents and would never find them again, to the father away at work, to her time alone in hospital with severe whooping cough which turned her blue.... A narrative dreamed by me is transformed into a sequence of narratives dreamed by the patient.

On the next Sunday night I sleep badly because of extremely irritating events in my personal life.

The next day I have sessions Simona and also with Silvia, and these turn out well.

On Tuesday I am sleepy again. Silvia has the following dreams: her dog, sleeping beside her, *seems to be crying*. Then she is back in her consulting room after an expensive shopping trip, and her colleague, who is with a patient, tells her there is an old man in the waiting room. He is trembling and wants to know who will be seeing him. Silvia tells him it's not her job to look after him. But why is the man trembling: with cold? with anger? She adds that her mother never goes to bed until late at night.

Simona dreams (connecting the two dreams to her father) that somebody has to retire from work and then that someone was aggressive and threatening on one level but calm and welcoming on a higher level.

Both patients have caught the bad state of my mental functioning (Silvia adds that she has met a threatening professor).

Silvia has reacted by dramatizing my distress and the fact that I was "trembling" with anger, showing that at this point there was no one taking care of her.

Simona has ironically caught my state of mind, suggesting its time I retired and grasping the dual state (welcoming/furious) I had been in – partly unconsciously – in the previous session.

Silvia begins the next session by telling me she doesn't understand her brother, who has so much faith in the world that he's had four children, and that some training analysts give three sessions a week.

I say, "Why doesn't yesterday's session count?"

I follow up with a partial self-disclosure in which I tell her that I hadn't got much sleep and wasn't on my best form. After a brief silence she tells me about refuse collection and how she thinks it's pointless separating all the different kinds of waste. Whatever needs to be thrown away gets thrown away in one go, without wasting time separating it all. Then she adds a joke about an analyst putting a carrot on the couch and saying, "I'm an expert 'in fields' too."

She goes on to talk about hedgehogs, prickly pears, sweet chestnuts: structures which have thorns or spines on the outside, but tender flesh on the inside, acknowledging *en passant* why these structures have had to equip themselves with spines and thorns.

Regurgitation of undreamed dreams: paranoid functioning

Patients in paranoid phases of functioning often evacuate their own emotions (or proto-emotional states) and then inspect every detail in search of the emotion-wolf which might attack them.

They lose the overall view, the completeness of a smiling face or a beautiful panorama, so as to spot the clue which would reveal where the wild beast is lurking. Discovering the detail would enable them to discover the wolf.

Let's put a mountain peak into a panorama: it might be "the projected fang of the wolf-emotion" which could tear the patient to pieces. From this derives the attention to every detail, every micro-signal, the suspicion of every rustling leaf which might enable the patient to discover and flee from all the projected emotions he fears will attack him.

Suspicion, the investigative stance, clothes him like a secret agent in search of the detail which would enable to discover where the danger is. He finds himself in a cowboy film when what looked like a hilly landscape turns out to have "plumes of smoke" which reveal the presence of savage Indians-emotions which might attack him, and he closes the circle of his wagons to keep out the emotions he has expelled.

The starting point is nevertheless the inadequacy of the container of emotional states, which are expelled and then go into hiding.

In the case of "paranoia", the presence of an archaic Superego, or rather of $-(\female\male)$ stops the wolves or bison being visible and having to mask themselves.

In the end, all the defence mechanisms (which we then call symptoms) are more or less successful attempts to withdraw from the (proto)emotions which tear and rend … or could do so.

Depending on the functioning of other constellations [♂♀, projective identification, Superego, −(♀♂)] one chosen symptom or another comes to the fore, and I would not consider the choice rigid or irreversible, but mobile and reversible, the more so the younger the patient is.

Another sort of primitive mental state ♂ that is expelled sometimes turns into bullying: where a mass of expelled bison becomes constantly threatening and one repeatedly succumbs to it.

Storylines for future dreams: first meetings

Claudia is a patient who asks for analysis because of an existential discontent, panic attacks, and worsening obesity which causes her shame and embarrassment.

She works in a group which manages the "adoption of abandoned dogs". She is also strictly vegan. Her father is described as violent, as was her first husband.

The scene which takes shape in my mind is that of a dual functioning: on the one had the "vegan", on the other the "werewolf" hidden between the folds of obesity, its ravenous violence masked by the "bloodless vegan". All the food she takes in (especially carbohydrates) seems to have the function of reining in the "werewolf" which must be placated by Pantagruelesque quantities of food.

She is married to a forest ranger whom she describes as a fine person who likes meat and "keeps corpses in the fridge" (being a meat-eater).

And so someone appears who knows how to manage the wolf and its carnivorous voracity. Claudia brings a dream to the first meeting, and it proves central: she is in a garden where she is attacked by a fierce Rottweiler and tries to defend herself but her flesh is torn. Then some people arrive to protect her.

What I had thought of as a werewolf is in fact a Rottweiler which tears at her: the vegan strategy of negation and the over-eating/obesity are confirmed. Over the course of the subsequent sessions the problem of why the Rottweiler is so furious becomes central. Has it been abandoned? Were its primary needs not acknowledged and met? It is certainly not ferocious for no reason. Before long a "refuge for ill-treated hounds" will come to life: the work goes on and Claudia opts for an analysis.

Eight-year-old Martina is brought for a consultation because some months ago she developed a number of tics, very intense and variable, and cannot bear storms, high winds, church bells, or even her doorbell at home.

The she starts to play games involving clashes between animals and between vehicles, as well as presenting a series of slight and changeable somatic manifestations.

It soon becomes obvious that her own entirely denied internal storms can only be evacuated in the tics and in mild psychosomatic manifestations.

She tends to keep a clear distance between herself and the conflictual and often violent contents (wearing roller-skates to sessions) or plays games in which she makes a rapid getaway from difficult situations. It is obvious that she is trying to escape from herself, but the split-off double we could call Martina 2 inexorably begins to take shape. At first, she appears in the titles of films she has seen on TV: *The Squall, The Storm, A Stranger at the Door.*

In work with children it is quite common to come across the "double" who can be considered the most likely precipitate of the suspended potential for identity.

Marzia, who has a stammer, is described as a faultless child: so I instantly find myself wondering about the "faulty" child who I feel must exist somewhere.

Then she talks about shadows that she sees and doesn't see, but which seem to follow her all the time. I think of a Pitbull starting to take concrete shape without her knowing it.

Then she tells me about moments when she's been very afraid of dogs, fearing that they will bite her.

In other words, she seems to live in an oscillation between a little Barbie doll and a Pitbull, and her stammer becomes the metaphorization of the red and green lights with which she holds back or lets go of her own emotions.

At this point she starts to be afraid of the "devil", who can be managed with the emergence of rituals of cleaning-exorcism.

Ludovica has been a perfect daughter for all of her fifteen years. When she was 13, she lost her mother to a serious illness.

For some time she has felt "strange presences" around her, finding support in this belief from her aunts who are attracted to the paranormal and participate in séances and such like.

Everything has gone smoothly until her first boyfriend, Mattia, appears on the scene. He is some years older, aggressive, violent, and comes from a criminal family. All the "shadows" seem to concretise in the form of Mattia (her mad part?).[7] He seems to fulfil the role of the "non-thing", that which is not metaphorizable in place of the void of a mourning which cannot be worked through. "Mattia" takes shape and comes to life with the function of an antidepressant. He gives her shoes which make her feel much taller, as if she were "three metres from the sky". He makes her feel loved, a princess.

She tells her version of a film she saw recently, which unfolds in four different stages: in the first there is a depressed woman who excites herself with sado-erotic fantasies; in the second, she cheers herself up by prostituting herself in a brothel; in the third, her depression disappears when she meets a violent characteropath who does not want to abide by the "house rules" of the brothel, but has the power to make her feel loved and no longer depressed; but – inevitably – in the fourth part, the woman's character flaw damages her family, bringing her loss and unhappiness.

As will be obvious, the patient is revisiting *Belle de Jour* and posing the problem of the sometimes revivifying use of the most diverse antidepressants and the possibly serious or very serious side-effects of such antidepressants.

An action as a missing (and recovered) dream

Francesca, a patient in the fifth year of analysis, arrives at 17.30, the correct time for her appointment, but I realise that I have been convinced that it's 18.30 and have set the rooms up for a supervision group which I have been holding at 18.30 for years. Not only that, I am convinced that she is a member of the group (who looks like her) and say, "Ciao." I notice my mistake immediately and the patient looks around the entrance hall in bewilderment at the completely different arrangement from usual: the chairs in a circle, the coat-stand in a different corner, other chairs added.

The patient understands my mistake and starts to talk about the absent-mind-edness and unreliability of her father who had gone out wearing his wife's hat by mistake, and so on.

I panic for a moment, thinking that nothing like that has ever happened to me; I think about getting senile, and how busy I am. Eventually I "see" the situation from another point of view: for some time the patient has been wondering about applying for this year's initial selection interviews. Of course, it's her decision, but am I giving her a green or red light in myself?

This is the answer: I am seeing the patient differently, as a colleague to whom I say "Ciao", someone I see in the context of supervision and not in analysis: my light is green.

The next day, the patient talks about major reorganisation going on in her workplace, and particularly about the need to repair the clocks which stopped long ago.

We reflect on the fact that the patient is in the fifth year of analysis and says that she feels ready to take the interviews. I tell her we'd have to move to New York for ten minutes, and so I make my partial self-disclosure before turning straight back to Europe.

The patient then tells me that she would begin her CV by saying, "I am the elder of two siblings".[8] I show her how it's time to stop being ambig-uous: she is a woman, not a man, and it is now time to leave behind all the ambiguities which have stopped her bringing her plans to fruition, including marriage and having a child. This would entail the rearrangement of the fur-niture in her house to make room for a future child's cot, and for her future patient's couch, I add.

I would like to stress in closing that I have gradually moved on from the idea that what the patient says is something I have to decipher, and have adopted other points of view, such as that of introducing the ever-stronger concept of relationship, then those of the field and of transformation in dream and in play.

These last two points of view, while remaining central to the way I operate (Ferro, 2009), continue to undergo adjustments. Now I try to work with the patient on how to carry out the job of directing or editing the narratives and sen-sorialities which have come to life, or are waiting to come to life, in the field.

Bion called one of his books *Taming Wild Thoughts*, but in my opinion, it is not a matter of taming them but of letting them live, and if it is normal to have *Little Women* and *Good Wives*, it is just as normal to be open to *Apocalypto*.

Every patient comes to us with characters not in search of an Author (we would be well on the way, in that case), but with a confused mass, a nebula of proto-somites, proto-devils, proto-Moriartys (Bion, 1975b) which have rarely arrived at being characters. If we already had Characters, we would be doing analyses which would be less challenging to our inventive-creative abilities (and by "our" I mean those of patient and analyst).

If a patient who is a well-respected surgeon comes to analysis and tells us he has grown a beard in order to distinguish himself from his brother who lives in the same city and is also a doctor, one who diagnoses non-existent cases of tuberculosis so as to "cure" his patients and become famous, and also tells us that his brother is about to embark on his seventh marriage, the first five wives having died of natural causes/illness/in accidents, while the sixth got away in time by divorcing him, it is not difficult to imagine various possible developments.

We could think of split-off aspects which will need a long transition in order to be integrated, in order to bring the model surgeon and the criminal doctor to the same table, rehabilitating the double, the imaginary twin, the secret companion.

But woe betide us, even in these cases, if we had such a storyline under development: we would be blinding ourselves to all the other possible stories, all the nebulae of beta elements which for the moment are clustered in that world and could be un-clustered to give rise – by re-clustering in a different way – to another possible world.

So, let's protect the film from having its development previewed prematurely.

A colleague had very correctly identified the theme of "narcissism" in a patient and had followed this thread, bringing the analysis to a good conclusion. Only a second analysis showed how many "interrupted paths", how many missed openings of other worlds, missed vivifications of incarcerated emotions there had been, culminating in a perpetual sense of suffocation with serious asthma attacks which brought the patient to seek the second analysis.

This is all the more the case when a patient presents with "zero character", and these people have to start putting out green shoots from a sort of desert. How do boredom, silence, repetition or extreme stupidity become *The Road, Crime and Punishment, The Silence of the Lambs, Anna Karenina*? Other examples can be found in clinical cases recounted at more length in my earlier books (Ferro, 2002b; 2003b; Ferro, et al., 2013).

There are analyses in which we start out with characters whom we think are the main ones, who may then confirm that they are, or may leave the stage; or unforeseen and unforeseeable characters may turn up.

With other analyses, where trust is required, we find ourselves in one of those Westerns where it's very hard to round up the herds running off in every direction, drive them to the river, persuade them to cross it in the direction of thinkability and then turn them into steaks, hamburgers, and fillets.

What is Anna's unthinkable world? One appropriate session follows another, and Anna is the kind of brilliant patient any analyst would like to have.

But who is Anna? What are Anna's other possible worlds? For now, she is a good actress ready to play the part for which the Actor's Studio has prepared her: an excellent patient!

What unexpressed potentialities could at some point start to gather? (including the equally possible one that – as Poe teaches in *The Purloined Letter* – that Anna is only Anna and nobody else!).

The *Star Trek* series comes to mind and how at a certain point it began to be populated by inhabitants of other worlds, physically very strange, almost para-doxical: so, we must make ourselves permeable to these "monsters" when and if they come, or like Bion in *Memoir of the Future*, to the somites, the Moriartys, the stegosauri, and so on.

So, I would say, let's lend one ear, to what the patient says, does, feels, but always keep another ear (or eye) open to the Nativity of something that was unthinkable/unthought before. Although not all patients ask this of us, they have the right to do so if they so wish: perhaps this is the difference between analysis and psychotherapy. Analysis is a journey, an adventure in search of the sources of the Nile: Indiana Jones, or the taste for travel and discovery. Psychotherapy is: I'm ill and I want to be better, but let's keep the work to a minimum. There is nothing to stop us switching from one path to the other at any moment.

Allowing for some invariants, I am multiple – some of these multitudes are prevalent, I would add for now, or *sic stantibus rebus*.

Other potentialities can come to life as in *I am Legend*, in the night, in the dark, and try to devour the dominant identities.

A patient had a fine grandmother, Eufemia, who was also a fine mother, a fine woman. She had brought up three moderately unhappy children, and in her kitchen she had the most gleaming aluminium that ever was seen (in her day, saucepans were made of aluminium and used to hang on display from the kitchen wall). Eufemia … she who speaks well, who is blessed.

But who was Granny Eufemia? She had a mobile kidney. She wore a truss to block the "mobile kidney" and if she put on a red truss, would it have become a wasp-waisted corset and would she have danced the Can-Can at the Moulin Rouge?

What else would that "kidney" have done, once it was no longer immobilised by the most containing truss that was ever seen?

But if a woman came to me for an analysis and told me about the problem with her mobile kidney, what worlds would be capable of opening up? And what if another patient rang me to say, "I live in Inganni".[9]

And what are we to say about a disturbing character from the childhood of another patient? Signora Giacometti, married to a scientist but militantly active in an ultra-orthodox Catholic-communist party, who ran off with a black jazz trumpeter and professional cardsharp. Would we have to "block" this mobile wasp's nest boiling with beta elements or, with the minimum of defences, open up as soon as possible a transformation from wasps to bees?

In a session a patient tells me he has dreamed about the caretaker of the resort where he spends his holidays, wearing his sunglasses the wrong way round, on his neck. I immediately think that the Sun is behind him, but what does that mean? That he feels the hour of sunset looming in front of him, or that he sometimes feels blinded by my too dazzling interpretations?

I have no way of knowing immediately, so we will see what itinerary prevails.

But, in the meantime, we see one of the functions of dream, or that of being a dream-catcher, or better still, of being an instrument capable of casting the characters who are not reachable in other ways. The dream has brought in the character "man with his sunglasses on his neck", the dream of the session which we will be able to have will enable us to locate and connect this character, and put together the film co-produced with the patient.

If a joke made by the analyst following a story about coins being switched for a plastic token in a supermarket, brings in the character the "swindler", maybe a sequence would come to life in which somebody wants to prevent (wants to swindle) his neck from seeing painful sights ... but this is only one of so many possible and speculative developments.... If the patient then says, "Today my father gave me lunch, and then the sun came out", it would be possible to hypothesise that the plotline has been confirmed (someone has transformed sensorialities into food) and the climatic conditions of the session would turn sunny. Thus, by trial and error, through a montage of rapid alternations between "stop" and "go", the dream of the session comes to life with one character whose casting was made by the patient's dream, another whose casting is derived from a rêverie, and another who is brought by the patient directly. In other words, first you have to go shopping (do the casting) and then cook the dream of the session.

Before the separation for the Christmas break, a patient says she has suffered a "sprain" and is in great pain ... and so pain enters the session. Then she adds that she has had a funny turn: in other words, the patient is saying, without knowing it, that she has been "given a funny turn" by the separation that is causing her pain. Naturally, all this will have to find a way of being embodied in a story that will go from transformative level *zero* ("You are telling me that you are angry and hurt") to transformative level Tn, depending on the degree to which the function of director/active cinematographer is engaged and able to develop not just the content but also the micro/macro-poietic capacity of the field.

It is sometimes possible to perform operations of pure decoding or arranging the pieces of a puzzle, but in these cases a lot of work has already been done, and the characters are only waiting for their organisation into narrative. Laura begins a session by talking about how well she is feeling, how content she is. Then she starts talking about two resuscitations for which she was called in as a consultant: a boy waiting for a heart transplant and a girl suffering from dyspnoea, running out of air as she waited for a lung transplant.

In this case, it seemed to me that we had enough elements (the patient had already provided "dream sequences") and so I felt able to say that, on the one hand, she was reminding me of the upbeat advertisement for a healthy snack for children, while on the other hand she seemed to be focusing on having heart trouble and feeling suffocated by something, something which was stopping her from fully inflating her lungs. From this point onwards, it is for the patient to develop these two strands which seem to be waiting for the availability of a road, a route along which to be unwound, so as to give shape to her dissatisfactions and doubts about her heart's choices and her need for freedom and autonomy.

Notes

1 *Marcellino, pan y vino* [Marcellino, bread and wine] a 1955 Spanish film directed by Ladislao Vajda. It tells of a poor orphan's miraculous relationship with a statue of Christ which comes to life.
2 Translator's note. Carla knows that her grandfather's innocent phrase is also gangster slang equivalent to "I'll wipe you out", "I'll waste you".
3 Translator's note: *Non ti muovere*, a prize-winning novel of 2001 by Margaret Mazzantini, made into a film of the same name by Sergio Castellitto.
4 Translator's note: *Un giorno dopo l'altro* is a novel by the popular singer, Guido Renzi]
5 Translator's note: "The woman from Ciociaria", a 1960 film by Vittorio De Sica released in the English-speaking world as *Two Women* and based on a novel by Alberto Moravia. The two women are gang-raped by Moroccan irregulars fighting with the French army during the Allied invasion of Italy in 1944.
6 Translator's note: German mercenaries widely employed in Italy during the 16th century. 14,000 of them were involved in the Sack of Rome in 1527.
7 Translator's note: the play is on "*matta*", mad.
8 Translator's note: Italian has no gender-neutral equivalent to "sibling" and so uses *fratelli* for both brothers and sisters. Hence, what Francesca literally says is "I am the elder of two brothers".
9 Translator's note: a district in Milan. *Inganni* also means "deceptions".

REFERENCES

Note: S. E. = The Standard Edition of the Complete Psychological Works of Sigmund Freud, trans. J. Stachey, London: Hogarth Press and the Institute of Psychoanalysis.Barale, F. and Ferro, A. (1992). Negative Therapeutic Reactions and Microfractures in Analytic Communication. In Nissim Momigliano, L. and Robutti, A. (Eds) *Shared Experience: The Psychoanalytic Dialogue*. London: Karnac Books.

Baranger, M. (1963). Bad Faith, Identity, and Omnipotence. In Baranger, M. and Baranger, W. (2009) *The Work of Confluence: Listening and Interpreting in the Psychoanalytic Field* (pp. 179–201). London: Karnac Books.

Baranger, W. and Baranger, M. (1961–1962). The Analytic Situation as a Dynamic Field. *International Journal of Psychoanalysis*, 89(4): 795–826.

Baranger, M. andBaranger, W. (2009). *The Work of Confluence: Listening and Interpreting in the Psychoanalytic Field*. London: Karnac Books.

Bertogna, C. (2014). Racconti. In Ferro, A.Mazzacane, F. and Varrani, E., *Con Nino Ferro: Supervisioni e creatività*.

Bezoari, M. (2014). The Dream Environment and the Analytic Environment. *Ital. Psychoanal. Annu.*, 8: 9–24.

BezoariM. and FerroA. (1999). The Dream Within a Field Theory: Functional Aggregates and Narrations. *Journal of Melanie Klein and Object Relations*, 17(2): 333–348.

Bing, E. (1976) *…ho nuotato fino alla riga*. Tr.it Feltrinelli, Milano1977.

Bion, W. R. (1963). *Elements of Psycho-Analysis*. London: Heinemann.

Bion, W. R. (1965). *Transformations*. London: Heinemann.

Bion, W. R. (1962). *Learning from Experience*, London: Heinemann.

Bion, W. R. (1970). *Attention and Interpretation*. London: Tavistock Publications.

Bion, W. R. (1975a). *The Dream. A Memoir of the Future*, Volume 1. London: Karnac Books.

Bion, W. R. (1975b). *The Past Presented. A Memoir of the Future,* Volume 2. London, Karnac Books.

Bion, W. R. (1978). Seminar held in Paris, July 10, 1978. Transcribed by F. Bion.

Bion, W. R. (1978b). *Bion in New York and Sao Paulo*. Perthshire: Clunie Press.

Bion, W. R. (1979a). *Making the Best of a Bad Job*. In *Clinical Seminars and Other Works*. London: Karnac Books.

Bion, W. R. (1979b). *The Dawn of Oblivion. A Memoir of the Future,* Volume 3. London: Karnac Books.

Bion, W. R. (1983). *The Italian Lectures.* London: Routledge.

Bion, W. R. (1987). *Clinical Seminars and Four other Papers.* Abingdon: Fleetwood Press.

Bion, W. R. (1992). *Cogitations.* London: Karnac Books.

Bion, W. R. (1997). *Taming Wild Thoughts.* London: Karnac Books.

Bion, W. R. (2005). *The Tavistock Seminars.* London: Karnac Books.

Bolognini, S. (2002a). *Psychoanalytic Empathy.* London: Free Associations Press.

Bolognini, S. (2002b). The Theoretical Models: Harmony and Coherence of the Psychoanalyst. Lecture held at the Theoretical Party FEP. Prague, April 2002.

Bonaminio, V. (2003). The Person of the Analyst. *Bulletin of the British Psychoanalytic Society,* 37: 28–42.

Borgogno, F. (2011). *The Girl Who Committed Hara-Kiri and Other Clinical and Historical Essays.* London: Routledge.

Brown, L. and Tarantelli, C. (2011). Personal communication.

Chianese, G. (1997). *Constructions and the Analytic Field. History, Scenes and Destiny.* London: Routledge.

Civitarese, G. (2008). *The Intimate Room. Theory and Technique of the Analytic Field.* London: Routledge.

Civitarese, G. (2011). *The Violence of Emotions: Bion and Post-Bionian Psychoanalysis.* London: Routledge.

Corrao, F. (1998). Il Concetto di Campo come Modello Teorico. In *Orme Vol II. Contributi alla Psicoanalisi.* Milano:Raffaello Cortina.

Di Chiara, G. (1978). Sulle finalità della psicoanalisi. Il valore delle costruzioni nell'analisi. Lecture given at the Psychoanalytic Centre of Milan.

Di Chiara, G. (Ed.) (1982). *Itinerari della psicoanalisi.* Torino: Loescher.

Di Chiara, G. (2003). Tracce, nessi, percorso dell'interpretare. In *Forme dell'interpretare.* Milano: Franco Angeli.

Faimberg, H. (1996). Listening to Listening. *International Journal of Psychoanalysis,* 77(4): 667–677.

Ferenczi, S. (1912). Transitory symptom-construction during the analysis. In *First Contributions to Psychoanalysis,* pp. 193–212. London: Hogarth.

Ferro, A. (1987). Il mondo alla rovescia. Inversione del flusso delle identificazioni proiettive. *Rivista di psicoanalisi,* 33(1): 59–77.

Ferro, A. (1992). *The Bi-Personal Field: Experiences in Child Analysis.* London: Routledge.

Ferro, A. (1996). *In the Analyst's Consulting Room.* Hove: Brunner-Routledge.

Ferro, A. (2002a). *Seeds of Illness Seeds of Recovery.* London: New Library/Routledge.

Ferro, A. (2002b). Some Implications of Bion's Thought: The Waking Dream and Narrative Derivatives. *International Journal of Psychoanalysis,* 83: 597–607.

Ferro, A. (2003a). Marcella from Explosive Sensoriality to the Ability to Think. *Psychoanalytic Quarterly,* 72: 183–200.

Ferro, A. (2003b). *Supervision in Psychoanalysis: The São Paulo Seminars.* London: Routledge, The New Library of Psychoanalysis.

Ferro, A. (2004). Realié des faits et realité interne: des derives narratifs aux émotions premières. In Chouvier, B. and Roussillon, R. (Eds), *La Réalité Psychique.* Paris: Dunod.

Ferro, A. (2005a). Which Reality in the Psychoanalytic Session? *Psychoanalytic Quarterly,* 74: 421–442.

Ferro, A. (2005b). Commentary on Field Theory by Madelaine Baranger and on the Confrontation between Generations as a Dynamic Field by Luis Kancyper. In Lewkowicz, S. and Flechner, S. (Eds), *Truth, Reality and the Psychoanalyst.* London: IPL.

Ferro, A. (2006a). Clinical Implications of Bion's Thought. *International Journal of Psycho-analysis*, 87: 989–1003.

Ferro, A. (2006b). *Mind Works: Technique and Creativity in Psychoanalysis*. London; New York: Routledge New Library.

Ferro, A. (2007). *Avoiding Emotions, Living Emotions*. London; New York: Routledge New Library.

Ferro, A. (2008). *Reveries: An Unfettered Mind*. London: Karnac Books.

Ferro, A. (2009). Transformations in Dreaming and Characters in the Psychoanalytic Field. *International Journal of Psychoanalysis*, 90: 2009–2030.

Ferro, A. (2010). *Torments of the Soul*. London; New York: Routledge New Library.

Ferro, A. (2012). *The Sao Paulo Seminars: Theory and Technique in Psychoanalytic Supervision*. London: Routledge.

Ferro, A. and Basile, R. (Eds) (2009). *The Analytic Field. A Clinical Concept*. London: Karnac Books.

Ferro, A., Mazzacane, F. and Varrani, E. (2015). *Nel Gioco Analitico*. Milano: Mimesis Edizioni.

Ferro, A., Civitarese, G., Collovà, M., Foresti, G., Mazzacane, F., Molinari, E. and Politi, P. (2007) *Sognare l'analisi. Sviluppi clinici del pensiero di Wilfred R. Bion*. Torino: Bollati Boringhieri.

Ferro, A., Civitarese, G., Collovà, M., Foresti, G., Mazzacane, F., Molinari, E. and Politi, P. (2011). *Psicoanalisi in Giallo: l'analista come detective*. Milano: Raffaello Cortina.

Ferro, A., Civitarese, G., Collovà, M., Foresti, G., Mazzacane, F., Molinari, E. and Politi, P. (2013). *Contemporary Bionian Field Theory and Technique in Psychoanalysis*. London: Routledge.

Ferruta, A. (2003). Trattare l'ambiente in termini di trasfert. Il concetto di interpretazione negli scritti di Winnicott. In Fabozzi, P., *Forme dell'interpretare*. Milano: Franco Angeli.

Ferruta, A. (2014). Personal communication.

Fonda, P. (2012). Ripensando il tessuto relazionale negli Istituti di Training. Lecture given at the Giornata sul Training, SPI, Milano, October, 2012.

Freud, S. (1909). Notes upon a Case of Obsessional Neurosis (Rat Man Case) Notes upon a case of obsessional neurosis. *S. E. 10*: 151–318.

Freud, S. (1914b). Remembering, Repeating and Working Through. *S. E. 12*: 145–156.

Freud, S. (1923–1925) Negation. *S. E. 1*: 235–239.

Freud, S. (1937). Analysis terminable and interminable. *S. E. 23*.

Frisch, S., Bleger, I. and Sechaux, E. (2010). La spécificité du traitement psychanayticque aujourd'hui. *Bulletin FEP*, 64: 95–122.

Gabbard, G. and Lester, E. P. (1995). *Boundaries and Boundary Violations in Psychoanalysis*. Washington, DC: American Psychiatric Publications Inc.

Gaburri, E. (1997). *Emozione e interpretazione. Psicoanalisi del campo emotivo*. Torino: Ed. E. Gabburi Bollati Boringhieri.

Green, A. (1989). *La pensée Clinique*. Paris: Odile Jacob.

Green, A. (2005). The Illusion of the Common Ground and Mythical Pluralism. *International Journal of Psychoanalysis*, 86: 627–632.

Greenberg, L. S. (2012). Personal communication.

Grotstein, J. (2007). *A Beam of Intense Darkness: Wilfred Bion's Legacy to Psychoanalysis*. London: Karnac Books.

Grotstein, J. (2009). *"But at Same Time, Another Level…": Psychoanalytic Theory and Technique in the Kleinian/Bionian Mode*. London: Karnac Books.

Laplanche, J. and Pontalis, J-B. (1967). *The Language of Psychoanalysis*. London: Karnac Books.

Leuzinger-Bohleber, M., Dreher, A. U. and Canestri, J. (2003). *Pluralism and Unity? Methods of Research in Psychoanalysis*. London: International Psychoanalytical Association.

Joseph, B. (1985). Transference: The Total Situation. *Psychic Equilibrium*: 157–158.

Junkers, G. (2013). *The Empty Couch: The Taboo of Ageing and Retirement in Psychoanalysis*. London: Routledge.

Meltzer, D. (1984). *Dream-Life*. Perthshire, UK: Clunie Press.

Neri, C. (2006). Campo. In Barale, F., Bertani, M., Gallese, V., Mistura, S. and Zamperini, A. (Eds), *Psiche. Dizionario storico di psicologia, psichiatria, psicoanalisi e neuroscienze*. Torino: Einaudi.

Nicolò, A. M. (2003). Utilità e limiti dell'interpretazione. In Fabozzi, P., *Forme dell'interpretare*. Milano: Franco Angeli.

Nissim Momigliano, L. (2001). *L'ascolto rispettoso. Scritti psicoanalitici*. Milano: Raffaello Cortina.

Nissim Momigliano, L. and Robutti, A. (Eds) (1992). *Shared Experience: The Psychoanalytic Dialogue*. London: Karnac Books.

Norman, J. (2001). The Psychoanalyst and the Baby: A New Look and Work with Infants. *International Journal of Psychoanalysis*, 82: 83.

Ogden, T. (1994). The Analytic Third: Working with Intersubjective Clinical Facts. *International Journal of Psychoanalysis*, 75: 3–20.

Ogden, T. (2007). On Talking as Dreaming. *International Journal of Psychoanalysis*, 88: 575–589.

OgdenT. (2009). *Rediscovering Psychoanalysis: Thinking and Dreaming, Learning and. Forgetting*. London: Routledge.

Petrella, F. (2011). *La mente come teatro*. Milano: Edi-ermes.

Renik, O. (1998). The Analyst's Subjectivity and the Analyst's Objectivity. *International Journal of Psychoanalysis*, 3: 487–497.

Riolo, F. (1997). Il Modello di Campo in psicoanalisi. In Gaburri, E. (Ed), *Emozione e interpretazione. Psicoanalisi del campo emotivo* [*Emotion and interpretation: psychoanalysis of the emotional field*]. Turin: Bollati Boringhieri.

Riolo, F. (2007). Psychoanalytic transformations. *International Journal of Psychoanalysis*, 88: 1375–1389.

Rocha Barros, E. (2000). Affect and Pictographic Image: The Constitution of Meaning In Mental Life. *International Journal of Psychoanalysis*, 81: 1087–1099.

Salomonsson, B. (2007). Talk to Me Baby, Tell Me What's the Matter Now. Semiotic and Developmental Perspectives on Communication in Psychoanalytic Infant Treatment. *International Journal of Psychoanalysis*, 88: 127–146.

Segal, H. (2007). *Yesterday, Today and Tomorrow*. London: Routledge.

Stern, D. (2013). Personal communication.

Tuckett, D., Basile, R., Birkstead-Breen, D., Bohm, T., Denis, P., Ferro, A., Hinz, H., Jemstedt, A., Mariotti, P. and Schubert, J. (2008). *Psychoanalysis Comparable and Incomparable. The Evaluation of a Method to Describe and Compare Psychoanalytic Approaches*. Hove: Routledge.

Wallerstein, R. S. (1988). One Psychoanalysis or Many? *International Journal of Psychoanalysis*, 69: 5–21.

Wallerstein, R. S. (1990). Will Psychoanalytic Pluralism be an Enduring State of our Discipline? *International Journal of Psychoanalysis*, 86: 623–626.

Widlöcher, D. (1996). *Les nouvelles cartes de la psychanalyse* [*Psychoanalysis: New Cards, New Approaches*]. Paris: Odile Jacob.

Williams, A. H. (1983). *Nevrosi e delinquenza*. Roma: Borla.

Winnicott, D. W. (1971). *Playing and Reality*. London: Routledge.

INDEX

Page numbers in italics refer to figures.

action, as missing dream 131–135
admissions procedures, for training analysis 67
age, and biomarkers 123
Alien (Scott) 68
alphabetisation 50, 56, 57, 58, 61, 89, 96–101, 124; casting characters 104–105; depression 109–115; disturbances in learning 103–104; evacuation 101–102; potential criminality 102–103; Row C of the Grid 105–109
alpha dreams 23
alpha elements 4, 10; evacuation of 55; redreaming of 23; transformation from beta elements into 23, 37–38, 57, 58, 70, 122
alpha functions 4, 11, 16, 34, 37, 49, 57, 59, 63, 70, 78, 79, 99, 101, 106; super alpha function 24, 38, 57
ambivalence 122
analysis: admissions procedures for training 67; training 21, 67, 110; as transitional space 15
analysts: dreams of 126; gifts of 18, 34; interpretative responses of 3; mental functioning of 4, 11, 18, 30; negative capabilities of 2, 13, 15–16, 22–27, 99; neutrality of 53–54; sexual actions between patients and 42–45; trainee 45–46; uniforms of 53

analytic field 10–11, 13, 59–62, 69, 97, 99–101; and analyst's mind 34–36; and characters 105; creativity of 20; emotional 16; and potential identities 119; pure 79; re-dreaming in 99
"analytic third" 23, 98
Apocalypto 132
Asperger's syndrome 76, 104
assertion 13, 14
attacks, on setting 126

Baranger, Madeleine 7–8, 13, 14, 56, 97
Baranger, Willy 13, 14, 56, 97
Bartleby the Scrivener (Melville) 14
Basile, Roberto 11
Beam of Intense Darkness, A (Grotstein) 98
benevolence 34
beta elements 7, 11, 18, 106; alphabetisation of 58; beta 1 98; beta 2 98; evacuation of 55, 57, 58; transformation to alpha elements 23, 37–38, 57, 58, 70, 122
biological markers, of time 123
Bion, W. R. 2, 3, 4, 8, 9–11, 13, 14, 15, 16, 18, 21, 23, 26, 29, 31, 33, 34, 36, 37–38, 45, 47, 52, 56–58, 74, 79, 86, 96, 97, 98, 99, 100, 101, 117, 124, 132, 133
blindness 34
Blue Angel, The (von Sternberg) 109
Bollain, Iciar 47
Bollas, Christopher 121

Botella, C. 98
Brown, Larry 79

Cabinet of Dr Caligari, The (Wiene) 36, 48–49
Carosello 62
casting, of characters 98, 104–105
celebrating the known 119–120
Chagall, Marc 18
characters 3, 11, 20, 40, 61, 64; affective holograms 11, 97; animated 62; casting 98, 104–105, 134; and elective mutism 64; as medications 66, 68; quality attributed to 30; and symptoms 88, 89; transformation of people into 100; zero character 132
circular time 51, 72–74
Cogitations (Bion) 96
comedy 82
communication 1, 2, 4, 9, 17–18, 50, 78, 90, 123, 126
communicative transgression 50
Conrad, Joseph 15, 24, 99
contents, and modalities 116–119
co-thinking 14, 53
creativity 16, 22–27, 46, 77, 101; of field 20; loci of 100, 119
culture 70

Dark at the End of the Tunnel (Bollas) 121
declarative memory 124
delirium 88
delusions 33, 48, 49, 68, 112, 119
denial 13, 14, 52; play/negative capabilities as antidote to 15–16; relational dimension 14
depression 40, 66, 68, 72, 109–115
derived narratives 57–58, 78
desire, listening without 2, 16
destructiveness 49
detective thrillers 80
Die leere Couch (Junkers) 73
discrimination, ability of 120
domestic violence 47–48
double 49–50
dream-listening, vertex of 47–53
dreams: alpha 23; of analysts 126; capacity for poetic syncretisation 86–87; difficult 116, 126–128; easy 116, 125–126; maps of *108*; missing, action as 131–135; night 23, 50; nocturnal 38; research, in psychoanalysis 37–38; as storylines for future 129–130; transformations in 18, 20, 59, 90, 97, 98, 99; undreamed 58,

101, 125, 128–129; *see also* waking dream-thought
dreaming 124–128; ensemble 4, 51, 58, 70, 79, 99; talking as 4, 46–47, 112, 121–122
dyslexia 56, 61, 88; emotional 62–64

"*Einfälle*" 4
elective mutism 61, 63–64
emotional grammar, basic 56, 59–62, 119
encyclopaedias 2
enuresis 56, 63
erectile dysfunction 88–89
erotic transference 43, 89
ethics 42–45, 99
evacuations 55–56, 63, 87–88, 101–102, 103; Bion 56–58; conversion *vs.* somatisation 57–58

Faimberg, Haydée 15, 28
fantasies 42, 44, 47, 112, 117, 130
fear 119–122; of not knowing 32; and psychoanalysis 51–53
femininity 5, 20, 108–109, 121, 122
Ferenczi, S. 15
Ferrandino, Giuseppe 103
Ferro, A. 87
field theory 9–11, 14
figurability 98
film noir 81
films 9–10, 47–53, 61, 68, 70, 77, 90, 91, 107, 117, 130
Fonagy, Peter 28
Fonda, Paolo 52
free associations 1, 4, 24, 37
Freud, Sigmund 1, 2, 3, 13, 14, 33, 39, 46, 50, 52, 124
fundamental rule 1–5, 11–12; clinical reflections 5–9; contributions from Bion and field theory 9–11
future: access to 10; dreams, as storylines for 129–130

Gabbard, G. 42
Galileo 33
games, verbal 21–22
genre 80–85; literary 23, 79, 117; narrative 4, 77, 117; visual-cinematic 117
Germany Year Zero (Rosselllini) 77
gifts, of analysts 18, 34
Good Wives 132
Green, A. 32, 96, 97
Greenberg, Jay 20, 21
Grotstein, J. 2, 3, 8, 10, 15, 24, 29, 47, 57, 58, 97, 98, 99
group supervision 75–77

hallucinations 7, 55, 87, 102–103
hallucinosis, transformation in 33, 36–37, 57, 87–88
hieroglyphic mother 118–119
history (genre) 82
Hitchcock, Alfred 125
Holmes, Sherlock 9
horror (genre) 83
Hugo, Victor 8
Hume, David 19
hyperbole 13
hyper-continence 56, 61, 63, 64, 102

I Am Legend (Lawrence) 68, 133
If on a Winter's Night a Traveller (Calvino) 116
images 57–58, 65–66
immutability 53
implicit memory 124
incontinence 56, 61, 63, 64, 102
individual supervision 78–80
insight 51
interpretation 3, 7, 94; narrative 14, 15; operations upstream of 22, 26; and patient confirmation 30, 34–36; patient's response to 15, 78; and rêverie 26; simplicity of 31
interpretative interventions 15, 78, 123, 126
interpretative line 16–20
interpretative responses, of analysts 3
Invasion of the Body-Snatchers, The (Siegel) 68
Italian Psychoanalytic Society 45

Junkers, Gabriele 73

Keats, John 13
Klein, Melanie 3, 79
knowledge 2, 18; and fear 51–52; not-knowing 19, 31, 32, 33, 52, 103

Lacan, Jacques 3
Lawrence, Francis 68
learning, disturbances in 103–104
Les Miserables 8–9, 74
Lester, E. P. 42
Leuzinger-Bohleber, M. 28
"Liar's Metaphor" 74
linear time 72–74
listening 2, 18; dream-listening, vertex of 47–53; interpretative line 16–20; magic filter 89–95, *93*; to unconscious 2–3; without memory and desire 2, 16
Little Women 132
loneliness 68

Lucretius 34, 100
lying 18, 39, 71–72, 74

magic filter 9, 89–95, *93*
Mann, Heinrich 109
Manzoni, Alessandro 34, 44
Meltzer, D. 33, 37, 57
Melville, Herman 14, 36
Memoir of the Future (Bion) 133
memory 101, 124; declarative memory 124; listening without 2, 16
mental functioning 60, 75–76, 88, 89; of analysts 4, 11, 18, 30; of patients 1, 11, 92, *93*, 116; and supervision 75–76
mentalisation 57, 58
metabolisation 16, 57, 58, 79
metaphors 2, 4, 10, 24, 26, 44, 63, 66–67
metapsychological research 29
Miracle of Marcellino, The 117
modalities, contents and 116–119
Molière 33
mutism 56; elective 61, 63–64

narcissism, of patients 14
narrative interpretations 14, 15
narrative(s) 65–66; cinematic 68; derivatives 18, 20, 23, 89, 99, 100; derived 57–58, 78; genres 77, 79, 80–84; modes 2, 117, 119; waking dream-thought, derivatives of 23, 24
naughtiness 49
negative capabilities, of analysts 2, 13, 22–27, 99; as antidote to denial 15–16
negative rêverie 4, 27, 30
negative transference 37, 43, 44
Nel gioco analitico (Ferro) 77
Neri, C. 57
neutrality, of analysts 53–54
night dreams 23, 50, 58
Nissim Momigliano, Luciana 15
nocturnal dreams 38
Norman, J. 59

O 8, 15, 22, 74, 97, 98, 122; alphabetising 71; and defences, dialectic between 16; subjectivation of 10, 24, 71–72
obligatory associations 4
Ogden, T. 3, 8, 10, 23, 24, 34, 57, 58, 97, 98, 99, 119, 121
olfaction 120
oneiric flashes 57, 87
oneiricisation 99, 124
originality 46, 53
orthodoxy 32–34
Other, the 32, 56, 91; mind of 26, 57, 58

Pabst, Georg Wilhelm 125
para-delusion 119
paranoid functioning 128–129
paranoid-schizoid (PS) position 2, 13
Path to the Nest of Spiders, The (Calvino) 51
patients: and analysts, sexual actions between 42–45; dishonest 7–9; interpretation and confirmation 30, 34–36mental functioning of 1, 11, 92, *93*, 116; narcissistic 14; questions of, answering 31; response to interpretation 15, 78
Peckinpah, Sam 77
Pericle il Nero (Ferrandino) 103
pictograms 23, 24, 57, 100
play: as antidote to denial 15–16; transformations in 21–22, 99
Poe, E. A. 133
poetic syncretisation, capacity of dreams for 86–87
porn 83–84
pre-analytic psychotherapy 22
Professor Unrat (Mann) 109
projective identification 36, 58, 60, 89
proto-emotions 6–7, 26, 27, 57, 63, 68, 88, 106, 129
psychoanalysis: fear and 51–53; models of 4, 31–32, 45, 52, 53, 79, 101; as "mystical science" 29; *see also* research, in psychoanalysis
psychoanalytic church 119–122
psycho-intellective pathologies 103
psychosomatic maladies 66–67
psychosomatic pathologies 5–6, 55, 58, 103
Purloined Letter, The (Poe) 133

questions of patients, answering 31

Rat Man, The 14
reality 16, 17, 20, 34, 35, 36, 77, 105, 113, 122, 125
Reed, Gail 96
relational model 4
Remembering, Repeating and Working Through (Freud) 124
repetition 119–120
repression 9, 51, 57; and denial 13; process, correction of 50
research, in psychoanalysis: current trends 28–29; dreams 37–38; Freud 40; metapsychological research 29; mind of analyst in the field 30, 34–36; orthodoxy and science 32–34; phobia about emotional contact 38; slowness of change 36; subjects 30–31; theory *vs.* practice 29–30; understanding various models/theories 31–32
Resnik, Salomon 21
rêverie 5, 15, 20, 23–24, 26, 38, 49, 60, 89, 98; capacity, of analysts 3; deficiency of 61, 79; forms of 58; negative 4, 27, 30
romance (genre) 80–81
Rosselllini, Roberto 77

Salomonsson, B. 59
science 29, 32–34
science fiction 81–82
Scott, Ridley 68
Sechaux, E. 28
Secret Sharer, The (Conrad) 15, 99
Secrets of a Soul (Pabst) 125
Segal, Hanna 51
self-disclosure 31, 36
self-esteem 68
self-harm 49
semantic nests 105
sensoriality 10, 55, 57, 58, 79; transformation into images 57; transformation to waking dream-thought from 23, 24
sentimental (genre) 83
sexual actions, between patients and analysts 42–45
sexual disturbances 88–89
sexuality, in sessions 89
Siegel, Don 68
Sigurtà, Renato 21
Spellbound (Hitchcock) 125
splitting 8, 13, 14, 59, 110
Star Trek series 133
Steiner, John 47
"stupidification" 103
subjects, research 30–31
super alpha functions 24, 57
supervision 110; exercises 76, 77, 84–85; group 75–77; individual 78–80; narrative genres 80–84
symptoms 10, 50, 55, 56, 89; expression of 76; relapse of 116–117; sexual 88; and undreamed dreams 58

Take My Eyes (Bollain) 47
talking, as dreaming 4, 46–47, 112, 121–122
Taming Wild Thoughts (Bion) 132
Tarantelli, Carol 79
Tarantino, Quentin 77
Tavistock Seminars (Bion) 21, 29, 36, 45, 124
therapeutic reactions, negative 14, 49
thinkability 11, 18, 58, 124, 132

thinking: co-thinking 14, 53; tools for 9, 11, 31, 50, 70, 84, 97, 99, 101
"3-Ds syndrome" 61–62
time 72–74
training: analysis 21, 67, 110; and fear 52–53; and originality 46; supervision *see* supervision; trainee analysts 45–46
transformations 20, 24, 55; constructive 49; in dreams 18, 20, 59, 90, 97, 98, 99; in hallucinosis 33, 36–37, 57, 87–88; narrative 11, 15; in play 21–22, 99; from sensoriality to waking dream-thought 23, 24
transitional space, analysis as 15
traumas 35, 79, 122
Truman Show, The (Weir) 70
trust 34
truth: and emotions 99; tolerable 8, 15, 18
Tuckett, D. 28

uncontainability 56, 61
un-disguising 120–122
undreamed dreams 101, 125; regurgitation of 128–129; and symptoms 58

uniforms, of analysts 53
unipersonal model *see* relational model
unison 16
unrepressed unconscious 98
unsaturated interpretation *see* narrative interpretations

verbal games 21–22
verbal squiggling 20–21
violence, domestic 47–48

waking dream-thought 4, 16, 18, 36, 37, 57, 89; transformation from sensoriality to 23, 24
Wallerstein, R. S. 32
war fiction 79
Weir, Peter 70
Widlöcher, D. 14
Wiene, Robert 48–49
Winnicott, D. W. 15, 20

Zelig syndrome 45
"zero character" 132